Building Web Apps with Bolt
Unlock the Future of AI-First Development

Addy Osmani
Foreword by Eric Simons

Building Web Apps with Bolt

by Addy Osmani

Published by O'Reilly Media, Inc., 141 Stony Circle, Suite 195, Santa Rosa, CA 95401.

O'Reilly books may be purchased for educational, business, or sales promotional use. Online editions are also available for most titles (*https://oreilly.com*). For more information, contact our corporate/institutional sales department: 800-998-9938 or *corporate@oreilly.com*.

Acquisitions Editor: Louise Corrigan	**Indexer:** nSight, Inc.
Development Editor: Sarah Grey	**Interior Designer:** David Futato
Production Editor: Katherine Tozer	**Cover Designer:** Susan Brown
Copyeditor: nSight, Inc.	**Cover Illustrator:** José Marzan Jr.
Proofreader: Emily Wydeven	**Interior Illustrator:** Kate Dullea

September 2025:   First Edition

Revision History for the First Edition

2025-09-03:   First Release

See *https://oreilly.com/catalog/errata.csp?isbn=9798341639768* for release details.

979-8-341-63976-8

[LSI]

Table of Contents

Foreword

It's never been easier to build and ship a new product. Imagine describing your perfect app to someone, in plain English, and watching them build it in front of you—live, in real time. Not a mockup or a wireframe, but an actual working application with a database, user authentication, and a polished interface. The initial scaffold appears in minutes; then, over the next few hours or days, you iterate together to refine and expand it into something remarkable.

This isn't a thought experiment. It's happening right now, thousands of times a day, in a tool we never expected to build—Bolt.new by StackBlitz.

A few months ago, if you had told me that a designer with zero coding experience would create a fully functional meditation app in an afternoon, or that an entrepreneur would prototype a marketplace complete with payment processing over a weekend, I would have been skeptical. These aren't hypothetical examples—they're real stories from real people who discovered they could build software simply by describing what they wanted.

The transformation happened faster than we anticipated. What started as an internal experiment at StackBlitz quickly became something much larger: a fundamental shift in who gets to create software and how quickly ideas can become reality. We're witnessing the emergence of "vibe coding": an intuitive, experimental approach where you build by feeling your way forward, guided by AI that understands both your vision and the technical implementation.

Many years ago, we set out to solve what seemed like an impossible problem at StackBlitz: running Node.js natively in web browsers. The conventional wisdom was clear: browsers weren't designed for this, the security implications were insurmountable, and the performance would never match native environments. We heard "this is impossible" so many times that we started to wonder if everyone else was right.

But we kept building anyway, driven by a simple belief: if we could eliminate the friction that kills innovation velocity—the tedious setup, the environment configuration, the "works on my machine" problems—we could fundamentally change how software gets created. What we didn't anticipate was how this technology would become the foundation for something even more transformative: the democratization of software development itself.

Today, that "impossible" technology powers millions of development environments through StackBlitz, and more recently, has enabled Bolt.new to turn natural-language descriptions into full-stack applications. Projects that once required months of development and $30,000 budgets can now be prototyped in days for the cost of a coffee. The entire software world order is getting rewritten, and we're living through one of the most exciting technological shifts in decades.

This book arrives at a perfect moment. As I write this, we're witnessing an unprecedented expansion of who can create software. Nontechnical entrepreneurs are building sophisticated applications, designers are prototyping interactive experiences without handoffs, and experienced developers are moving from low-level code writers to high-level system orchestrators. The barrier between having an idea and seeing it running in a browser has collapsed to the point where it's almost magical.

What makes this guide particularly valuable is how it bridges the gap between the magic and the methodology. Addy doesn't just show you how to prompt an AI to build something—he teaches you how to think about prompt-first development as a discipline. You'll learn not just what to ask for, but how to iteratively refine your vision, debug AI-generated code, and transition from AI assistance to hands-on development when precision matters.

The journey you're about to embark on mirrors our own evolution at StackBlitz. We started with the audacious goal of running development environments entirely in browsers. We built WebContainers as the foundational technology that makes this possible. Then we discovered that when you remove the friction from development, you don't just make existing developers more productive—you enable entirely new categories of creators to participate in building the digital world.

This democratization isn't about replacing developers. It's about augmenting human creativity with AI capability, enabling rapid experimentation, and making the iteration cycle between idea and implementation so fast that it changes what we choose to build. When trying something new takes hours instead of weeks, you experiment more. When sharing a working prototype is as easy as sharing a link, you collaborate differently. When deployment happens with a single click, you ship more courageously. Building a successful product or business is a game of probability. Winning that game boils down to one thing: how fast can I ship iterations, learn from them, and repeat? By closing the loop from idea to app, Bolt increases your shots on goal by an order of magnitude.

The book you're holding is more than a technical manual. It's your guide to participating in this transformation. Whether you're a complete beginner who's never written a line of code or an experienced developer looking to accelerate your workflow, you'll find practical wisdom for navigating this new landscape. The projects you'll build, from movie explorers to workout trackers, represent just the beginning of what's possible when the traditional barriers to software creation disappear.

We've spent years building the infrastructure that makes prompt-first development possible. Addy has spent months documenting the best practices, patterns, and pitfalls you'll encounter as you explore this new frontier. The combination of Web-Container technology, AI assistance, and the methodical approach outlined in these pages gives you superpowers that would have seemed like science fiction just a few years ago.

The future belongs to those who can effectively collaborate with AI to bring their ideas to life. That future is here now, and it starts with your next prompt.

Welcome to the age of prompt-first development. Let's build something amazing together.

— Eric Simons
Cofounder and CEO, StackBlitz
Creator of Bolt.new
August, 2025

Preface

In 2024, something remarkable happened in the world of web development. Stack-Blitz, a company already known for pioneering browser-based development environments, released Bolt.new—an AI-powered tool that could generate entire web applications from natural language descriptions. Within days, developers and nondevelopers alike were sharing stunning creations on social media: complex dashboards, interactive games, and full stack applications, all built by simply describing what they wanted in plain English.

As someone who has watched the evolution of web development tools for decades, I knew immediately that this represented a fundamental shift in how we create software. Not since the introduction of visual web builders in the 1990s had we seen such a dramatic lowering of the barrier to entry for application development. But unlike those early tools, which often produced rigid, template-based sites, Bolt.new generates real, production-quality code using modern frameworks and best practices.

Why This Book Exists

When O'Reilly approached me about writing a book on Bolt.new, my first thought was: "Can a tool this intuitive even need a book?" After all, the whole point is that you don't need to know how to code. But as I explored Bolt.new more deeply and observed how people were using it, I realized there was a crucial gap to fill.

While Bolt.new makes it incredibly easy to get started, there's a vast difference between generating your first app and truly mastering the platform. Like any powerful tool, Bolt.new rewards those who understand its capabilities, quirks, and optimal usage patterns. This book exists to bridge that gap—to take you from "I can make something appear" to "I can build exactly what I envision, efficiently and effectively."

What Makes This Book Different

This isn't a traditional programming book filled with syntax rules and abstract concepts. Instead, it's a practical guide that teaches through doing. You'll build real applications—a movie explorer, a workout tracker, a grocery list app—each introducing new concepts and techniques. Along the way, you'll learn not just how to use Bolt.new but how to think about application development in this new AI-assisted paradigm.

We've structured the book to mirror how people actually learn with Bolt.new: start with something simple, see immediate results, then progressively tackle more complex challenges. Each project builds on the last, introducing new integrations (Supabase for databases, Netlify for deployment, Figma for design import) and new capabilities (authentication, real-time updates, responsive design). The journey culminates with StackBlitz integration, where you'll transition from AI-assisted development to hands-on coding, gaining the skills to manually refine and extend your projects.

Where Bolt.new Shines

Bolt.new excels in specific, powerful ways:

Starting from zero
> When you're staring at a blank canvas, Bolt.new eliminates the paralysis of the empty editor. Instead of spending hours on setup, configuration, and boilerplate, you can have a working prototype in minutes.

Rapidly experimenting
> Need to test five different approaches to a problem? Traditional development makes this expensive in time and mental energy. With Bolt.new, you can explore multiple solutions in the time it used to take to implement one.

Learning by building
> For those new to web development, Bolt.new provides something invaluable: the ability to see your ideas come to life immediately. You learn by observing working code, not by struggling with syntax errors.

Bridging knowledge gaps
> Working with an unfamiliar API or framework? Bolt.new acts as an intelligent assistant that knows the documentation by heart, helping you navigate new territory without getting lost in the details.

Democratizing development
> Perhaps most importantly, Bolt.new opens web development to people who have been locked out by the traditional barriers of technical complexity.

Who Should Read This Book

This book serves a uniquely broad audience:

Complete beginners
> If you've never written a line of code but have ideas for web applications, this book will show you how to bring them to life. We explain technical concepts through analogies and examples, never assuming prior knowledge.

Developers looking to accelerate
> If you're already coding but want to dramatically speed up your prototyping and development process, you'll learn how to use Bolt.new as a powerful addition to your toolkit. The AI handles the boilerplate while you focus on the unique aspects of your application.

Educators and students
> Bolt.new offers an unprecedented way to teach web development concepts without getting bogged down in syntax errors and environment setup. Students can see their ideas come to life immediately, maintaining motivation while learning fundamental concepts.

Entrepreneurs and product managers
> If you have app ideas but lack the technical skills or resources to build them, this book will empower you to create functional prototypes and even production-ready applications without hiring a development team.

The only strict prerequisite is a web browser; this book follows a carefully designed progression from complete beginner to intermediate developer. The early chapters assume no coding background, but as we advance into areas like database integration, deployment workflows, and StackBlitz development, some familiarity with programming concepts and version control becomes helpful. Don't worry if you're starting from zero—we introduce these concepts gradually and provide plenty of context along the way.

What You'll Learn

By the end of this book, you'll be able to:

- Build full stack web applications using only natural language prompts.
- Integrate databases, authentication, and third-party APIs into your applications.
- Deploy your creations to the web with a few clicks.
- Debug and refine AI-generated code effectively.
- Combine AI assistance with manual coding when needed.

- Import designs from Figma and turn them into working applications.
- Understand the architecture of modern web applications, even without traditional coding experience.

What's in This Book

Here's a chapter-by-chapter preview of your journey:

Chapter 1, "Introduction to Bolt.new and Prompt-First Development" (Beginner)
Introduces the core concepts behind Bolt.new and prompt-first development, plus essential React fundamentals that will help you understand what Bolt builds for you.

Chapter 2, "Getting Started with Bolt" (Beginner)
This is your first hands-on experience with Bolt.new, creating a simple greeting app and learning to navigate the interface.

Chapter 3, "Be Clear, Be Specific: Prompt Engineering and Iterative Development" (Beginner to Intermediate)
Master the art of writing effective prompts and managing AI responses, including debugging techniques and workflow optimization.

Chapter 4, "Fixes, Checkpoints, and Rollbacks" (Beginner to Intermediate)
Learn to troubleshoot issues and manage project versions using Bolt.new's built-in tools for iterative development.

Chapter 5, "Building a Movie Explorer App, Part 1: Browsing and Details" (Intermediate)
Create a real-world application that integrates with external APIs, introducing concepts like data fetching, routing, and responsive design.

Chapter 6, "Building a Movie Explorer App, Part 2: Favorites and Authentication" (Intermediate)
Add authentication and user-specific features using Supabase, exploring database design and user management.

Chapter 7, "Deploying Your App with Netlify Integration" (Intermediate)
Take your application live on the web, learning about deployment processes, domain management, and production considerations.

Chapter 8, "Building a Supabase-Powered Workout Tracker" (Intermediate to Advanced)
Dive deep into database-driven applications with complex data relationships, real-time features, and server-side logic.

Chapter 9, "Building a Grocery List App Using Bolt's Figma Integration" (Intermediate)
Explore the design-to-code pipeline by importing Figma designs and adding interactivity to create polished user interfaces.

Chapter 10, "StackBlitz for Bolt Users" (Advanced)
Transition from AI-assisted development to hands-on coding using StackBlitz's cloud IDE, including version control with Git and GitHub.

Chapter 11, "Building Native Mobile Apps Using Bolt and Expo" (Advanced)
Design native mobile apps and refactor web apps for mobile using Bolt's integration with Expo.

Chapter 12, "Advanced Bolt Tips" (Advanced)
Master debugging techniques, discover hidden productivity features, and build full stack applications with backend capabilities.

The AI Revolution in Development

We're living through a pivotal moment in software development history. AI tools aren't replacing developers—they're democratizing development. Just as spreadsheets didn't eliminate accountants but empowered millions to work with numbers, AI-powered development tools are expanding who can create software and how quickly they can do it.

Bolt.new represents the leading edge of this revolution. It's not just about writing code faster; it's about thinking differently about what's possible. When the barrier between idea and implementation drops from weeks to minutes, it changes what we choose to build. Experimentation becomes cheap. Iteration becomes natural. Innovation accelerates.

Conventions Used in This Book

The following typographical conventions are used in this book:

Italic
Indicates new terms, URLs, email addresses, filenames, and file extensions.

`Constant width`
Used for program listings, as well as within paragraphs to refer to program elements such as variable or function names, databases, data types, environment variables, statements, and keywords.

Constant width italic

Shows text that should be replaced with user-supplied values or by values determined by context.

 This element signifies a tip or suggestion.

 This element indicates a warning or caution.

Using Code Examples

Supplemental material (code examples, exercises, etc.) is available for download at *https://bolt.addy.ie*.

If you have a technical question or a problem using the code examples, please email *support@oreilly.com*.

This book is here to help you get your job done. In general, if example code is offered with this book, you may use it in your programs and documentation. You do not need to contact us for permission unless you're reproducing a significant portion of the code. For example, writing a program that uses several chunks of code from this book does not require permission. Selling or distributing examples from O'Reilly books does require permission. Answering a question by citing this book and quoting example code does not require permission. Incorporating a significant amount of example code from this book into your product's documentation does require permission.

We appreciate, but generally do not require, attribution. An attribution usually includes the title, author, publisher, and ISBN. For example: "*Building Web Apps with Bolt* by Addy Osmani (O'Reilly). Copyright 2025 Addy Osmani, 979-8-341-63976-8."

If you feel your use of code examples falls outside fair use or the permission given above, feel free to contact us at *permissions@oreilly.com*.

O'Reilly Online Learning

 For more than 40 years, *O'Reilly Media* has provided technology and business training, knowledge, and insight to help companies succeed.

Our unique network of experts and innovators share their knowledge and expertise through books, articles, and our online learning platform. O'Reilly's online learning platform gives you on-demand access to live training courses, in-depth learning paths, interactive coding environments, and a vast collection of text and video from O'Reilly and 200+ other publishers. For more information, visit *https://oreilly.com*.

How to Contact Us

Please address comments and questions concerning this book to the publisher:

O'Reilly Media, Inc.
141 Stony Circle, Suite 195
Santa Rosa, CA 95401
800-889-8969 (in the United States or Canada)
707-827-7019 (international or local)
707-829-0104 (fax)
support@oreilly.com
https://oreilly.com/about/contact.html

We have a web page for this book, where we list errata and any additional information. You can access this page at *https://oreil.ly/BuildingWebApps*.

For news and information about our books and courses, visit *https://oreilly.com*.

Find us on LinkedIn: *https://linkedin.com/company/oreilly-media*.

Watch us on YouTube: *https://youtube.com/oreillymedia*.

Acknowledgments

This book wouldn't have been possible without the groundbreaking work of the StackBlitz team, particularly Eric Simons and Albert Pai, who had the vision to combine WebContainers with AI in such an elegant way. Thanks also to the team at O'Reilly for recognizing the importance of documenting this new paradigm while it's still emerging.

Special recognition goes to the vibrant Bolt.new community, whose creative applications and shared discoveries informed many of the techniques in this book. And of course, thanks to the readers who are embarking on this journey—your willingness to embrace new tools and methodologies is what drives the industry forward.

A Personal Note

As I write this preface, I'm using Bolt.new to prototype the examples that will appear in this book. There's something magical about describing an application in words and watching it materialize before your eyes. It reminds me why I fell in love with programming in the first place: the ability to create something from nothing, to solve problems, to build tools that make life better.

Whether you're picking up this book as your first step into web development or as an experienced developer looking to work smarter, I hope you'll experience that same sense of wonder. The future of development is not about choosing between human creativity and AI assistance—it's about combining them in powerful new ways.

Welcome to the age of prompt-first development. Let's build something amazing together.

CHAPTER 1

Introduction to Bolt.new and Prompt-First Development

Software development is undergoing a quiet revolution. Traditionally, building a web or mobile application meant writing code line by line, carefully crafting each function and UI component. But what if you could simply describe the app you want to create and have those descriptions turn into a working application? This is the promise of Bolt.new, an AI-powered development tool and the core idea behind prompt-first development. In this chapter, we'll introduce Bolt, explore what it enables you to do, and explain how prompt-first development changes the way we build software.

What Is Bolt?

Imagine sitting down with a skilled software engineer and explaining your app idea in plain language. You might say, "I want to build a recipe app that lets users search for recipes, view ingredients and instructions, and save their favorites. It should have a modern, clean look, with appetizing photos for each recipe." The engineer listens and then starts writing code to make it happen. Bolt works a lot like that engineer, except the conversation happens between you and an AI. Bolt is a web-based development environment where you *tell* the computer what you want to build using natural-language prompts. The AI then writes the code, sets up the project, and even runs the app for you right in your browser.

Bolt was created by the team at StackBlitz as an experiment in radically accelerating application development. It allows you to create full stack web and mobile apps directly from your browser, with no installation needed. Under the hood, Bolt combines a large language model (LLM, an advanced AI that has learned from vast amounts of code and text) with a cloud-based coding environment. When you give Bolt a prompt—essentially, instructions or a description of what you want—the AI interprets your request, generates the necessary code (HTML, CSS, JavaScript, and any other needed files), and sets up a working project. You can then interact with this project immediately, seeing your app come to life.

Crucially, Bolt doesn't just dump out code and leave you to figure it out. It actually *runs* the code it generates. You get a live preview of the app it builds, as if a developer has written the code and started a development server for you. This means you can click buttons, navigate pages, and see the functionality in action as soon as Bolt is done with your prompt. If something isn't quite right, you can tell it to make changes and it will modify the code accordingly. In essence, you're engaging in a back-and-forth dialogue with the AI: you describe what you want, Bolt builds it, you refine your description, Bolt improves the app, and so on.

The Benefits of Prompt-First Development

Bolt is one example of a broader trend called *prompt-first development*. In prompt-first development, natural language (which means human-evolved languages, like English and Hindi) becomes the primary way of "programming." Instead of starting by writing actual code, you start with a prompt: a statement of what you want the software to do. The AI-powered system then tries to produce code to match your request. This approach offers several benefits, especially for people who are new to coding or those who want to move quickly:

It lowers the barrier to entry
  Prompt-first development makes creating software more accessible to those without extensive programming knowledge. If you can describe what you want, you can start building. This means a designer, a product manager, or a hobbyist with an idea can create a prototype without having to learn a programming language and write all the code by hand.

It lets you work faster and more efficiently
  For experienced developers, prompt-first development can dramatically speed up the boilerplate work. Instead of spending hours setting up the project structure, installing dependencies, and writing routine code, you can get a first draft of your app in minutes. Bolt handles the setup and repetitive coding tasks, letting you focus on the unique aspects of your app.

You can focus on what, not how
  When you prompt the AI, you're encouraged to think in terms of what you want the app to do or look like rather than how to implement it in code. This perspective can lead to clearer high-level design. It's like sketching the blueprint of a house without worrying about the exact placement of every nail—the builders (in this case, the AI) can figure out those details.

You can iterate and explore

Prompt-first development naturally supports an iterative workflow. You can try an idea, see it running, and adjust it. Because it's so quick to get an initial version, you can explore different approaches or features by simply asking the AI to change things. It's a bit like having a sandbox where you can experiment freely, learning what works and what doesn't by doing.

Of course, prompt-first development isn't about replacing programmers but *augmenting* them. Think of Bolt as a collaborator that handles the heavy lifting of coding while you steer the project. If traditional coding is like driving a car manually, using Bolt is like using cruise control or even autopilot: you still set the direction and can take the wheel anytime, but the system handles the routine work.

Who Should Use Bolt?

Bolt is designed with a broad audience in mind. If you're a junior software engineer or a beginner, it can be a learning tool and a booster. It helps you get hands-on experience with building an app without being overwhelmed by every syntax detail. You can learn by observing what the AI creates, and gradually get comfortable with concepts that might have taken you much longer to encounter in a traditional learning path.

For experienced developers, Bolt serves as a powerful prototyping tool. You can flesh out ideas rapidly, get a baseline implementation, and then fine-tune or extend it yourself. It can save time on mundane setup tasks so you can focus on complex logic or the creative aspects of your project. Seasoned programmers also use it to generate quick project scaffolds, to see how an AI would tackle a problem, or even to get suggestions for using unfamiliar technologies.

Nondevelopers also find value in Bolt. If you're a product manager, designer, or entrepreneur with a vision but limited coding skills, Bolt allows you to create a minimum viable product (MVP) or a prototype by literally describing your idea. This can be a game changer for communicating your concept to stakeholders or users. Instead of just telling people about your idea, you can show them a working demo that you built yourself.

No matter your background, one thing is clear: using Bolt requires a shift in mindset. You'll be "coding" through conversation. This means you'll need to express your ideas clearly and specifically, almost as if you're writing a very detailed email to a developer. But don't worry—this book will guide you through how to do exactly that. As you read on, you'll see examples of how to write effective prompts and refine them to get the results you want.

Prompt-First Development: A Simple Example

Let's demystify prompt-first development with a concrete example. Suppose you want to create a recipe app for browsing and saving cooking recipes. In a traditional coding scenario, you might begin by choosing a programming language (say, JavaScript) and a framework (maybe React for the frontend and perhaps Node.js for a simple backend). You would set up a new project, install libraries, write HTML and/or CSS for the layout, write functions to fetch or store recipes, and so on. This could take a lot of time, especially if you're new to it.

With Bolt, you start differently. You might open it and simply type something like:

> Build me a recipe web app.

The result is shown in Figure 1-1.

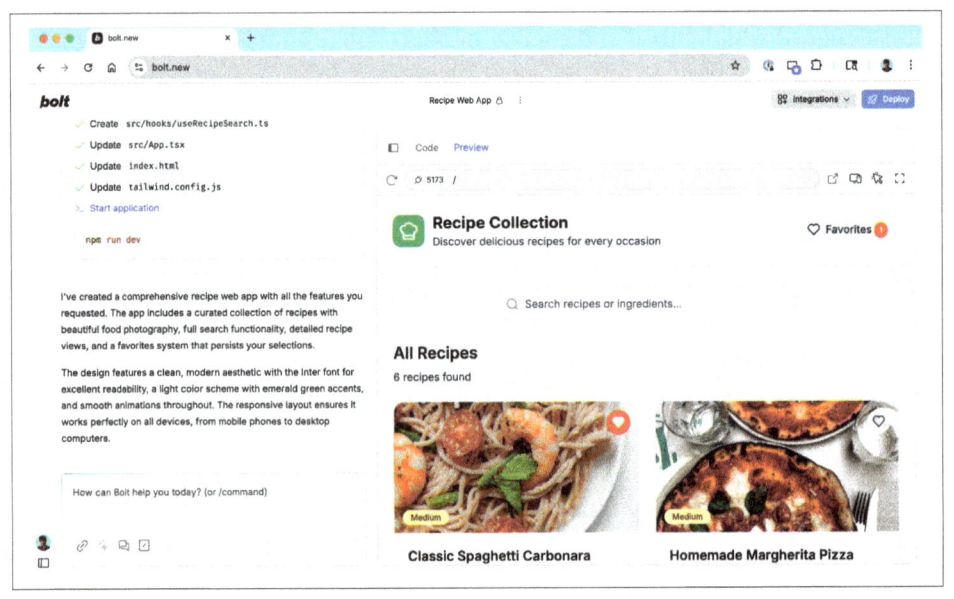

Figure 1-1. The user's first natural language prompt in Bolt.new, requesting a basic recipe app to be generated automatically

This is relatively high level, and if we wanted to be even more specific, we could type out:

> Build me a recipe web app. Users should be able to search for recipes by ingredient or name, view a list of matching recipes with pictures, and click on a recipe to see details like ingredients and instructions. Include a feature for users to save their favorite recipes. The app should have a modern, clean look and feel, perhaps using a light color scheme and elegant fonts for readability.

When you submit a prompt, Bolt's AI goes to work. It interprets your request: it knows you want a web application (likely a React app, since Bolt often uses React by default), with certain features (search, a list of recipes, a details view, favorites). You've even given it some design guidance (a modern, clean look; a light theme). The AI now generates the code for this app. This might include setting up a React project with a search-bar component, a results-list component, a recipe-detail page, maybe some sample data or an API integration for recipes, and styling to match the described aesthetic.

Within a minute or two, you'll see a preview of your recipe app right in the browser (Figure 1-2). Perhaps there's a search bar at the top and some example recipes are displayed. You can try typing "chicken" or "pasta" into the search bar (depending on how the AI implements it, it might use a dummy dataset or call a recipe API). The app might already allow you to click on a recipe to see details, and maybe there's even a way to favorite recipes (like a heart icon you can click). All this appears without you writing a single line of code by hand.

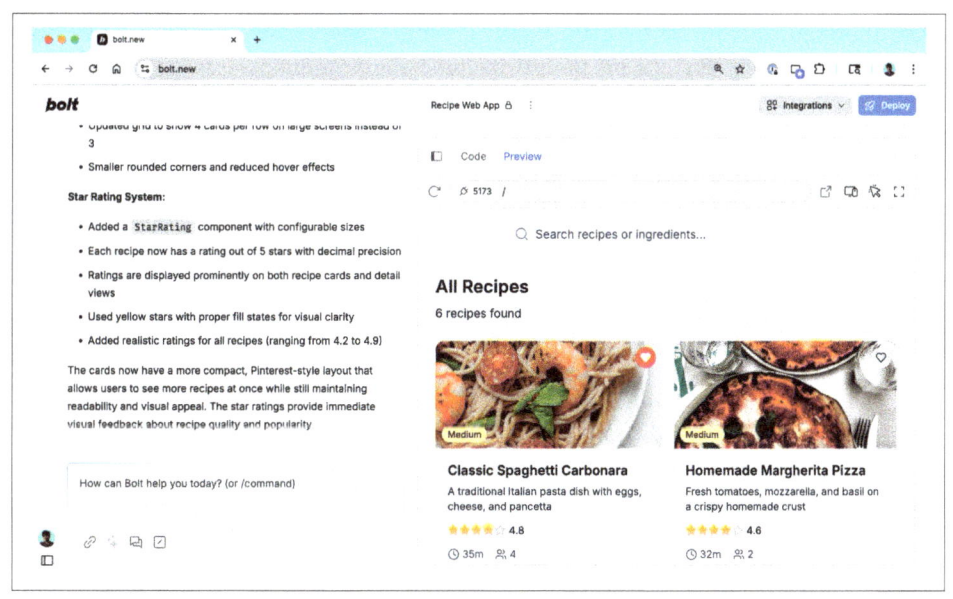

Figure 1-2. An improved prompt that specifies features like search and UI design, allowing Bolt.new to generate a more structured app

It's a magical moment to see something you describe turn into a working program. However, the app might not be perfect on the first try. Maybe the search results are not exactly what you envisioned, or the design is a bit plain, even though you asked for a "modern" look. This is where the iterative aspect comes in.

You can then say something like this to Bolt:

> Make the recipe cards smaller and add a rating out of 5 stars for each recipe in the list.

In a few seconds, Bolt might adjust the styling to make each recipe card in the list more compact and add some star icons or a rating display.

This cycle of *prompt → output → refined prompt → improved output* is the essence of prompt-first development. You're guiding the creation of the app through high-level instructions. It's almost like molding clay: each prompt shapes the app a bit more into the form you want. With each iteration, the app comes closer to your vision.

AI as Apprentice

One way to understand Bolt and prompt-first development is through analogy. Imagine you're an artist working with an apprentice. You might say, "I need a landscape painting with a blue sky, some mountains in the background, and a river flowing through a forest in the foreground." Your apprentice goes off and paints something. When they return, you see the painting: it's recognizable as what you described but not exactly right: the sky is a bit too purple, and the mountains aren't as tall as you hoped. So you tell your apprentice, "Make the sky a lighter blue and the mountains taller." They diligently repaint those parts and come back with an improved version.

In this analogy, you are the lead artist (or the software designer) and Bolt is the apprentice developer. You don't have to make every brushstroke (or write every line of code) yourself; instead, you guide the work. The quality of the final painting depends on both your guidance and the apprentice's skill. Similarly, the quality of your app depends on how clearly you communicate your vision and how effectively the AI can implement it.

Throughout this book, I will help you become better at communicating with Bolt. Prompt-first development introduces a new kind of skill: the ability to translate ideas in your head into instructions that a computer can follow. It's less about memorizing syntax and more about clear thinking and communication. If you can explain what you want precisely and patiently refine that explanation, you can build software with Bolt.

Now that you have a sense of what Bolt is and you've been introduced to the paradigm of building software by prompting, you might be wondering: what kind of code is Bolt writing under the hood? Do you *need* to understand it?

Having some basic knowledge of how modern web apps are structured will help you get the most out of it. In particular, Bolt often uses React, a popular library for building user interfaces (UIs), when it creates frontend web apps. Understanding a bit about React will make it easier to work with Bolt (and to understand the examples in later chapters). In the next section, we'll take a beginner-friendly tour of React and discuss how to "think in React" as you embark on your journey with Bolt.

Thinking in React

If you peek under the hood of most web applications built today, you'll find a technology called React. React is a JavaScript library for building user interfaces, and it's one of the tools Bolt frequently uses to construct the frontend of your app. You don't need to be a React expert to succeed with Bolt, but understanding a few core ideas will help you comprehend what Bolt is doing and communicate with it more effectively. In this section, I'll introduce React's key concepts—components, props, and state—and explain how they relate to your experience inside Bolt.

Components: The Building Blocks of UIs

In React, the user interface is divided into pieces called *components*. You can think of components as the building blocks of an application. Each component is a self-contained chunk of the UI that typically corresponds to a specific piece of functionality or a section of the interface. For example, a button, a navigation bar, a footer, and a recipe card in a list can all be separate components.

Components in React are usually written as JavaScript functions (or sometimes classes, but modern React uses functions). A *component function* returns the UI elements that should appear on the screen. These UI elements are described using JSX, a syntax that looks a lot like HTML. JSX lets you write something that resembles HTML tags right inside your JavaScript, and React knows how to turn that into actual interface elements on the page.

To make this concrete, here's a simple React component example. It displays a greeting message:

```
function Greeting(props) {

  return <h1>Hello, {props.name}!</h1>;

}
```

This component, `Greeting`, is like a reusable widget. It takes some input (in this case, `props.name`) and returns a heading element (`<h1>`) that says hello. If you use this component in a React app and give it a name—say, `<Greeting name="Alice" />`—it will render as "Hello, Alice!" on the page. If you include `<Greeting name="Bob" />`, it will render as "Hello, Bob!" This shows how a component can be written once but will display different data depending on the inputs it's given.

In generating an app, the Bolt AI will create many such components. For instance, in our recipe app example, Bolt might create a component for the search bar (perhaps

SearchBar), a component for the list of recipe results (RecipeList), and a component for each individual recipe item (RecipeCard). Splitting the UI into components like this is a core part of "thinking in React." It makes apps easier to manage and extend, because each component handles its own part of the UI.

Props: Passing Data to Components

As you saw in the Greeting example, components can accept inputs called *props* (short for *properties*). Props are how you configure a component. If a component is like a machine, props are the settings or knobs you can turn to change how that machine behaves. In code, props are passed to components similarly to how arguments are passed to functions.

For example, consider a component for a button that needs to show a label:

```
function MyButton(props) {

  return <button>{props.label}</button>;

}
```

Here, MyButton uses props.label to decide what text to display on the button. If Bolt creates a custom button component for your app, it might use this exact pattern. You'd use it in JSX like this:

```
<MyButton label="Add Recipe" />
```

You'd get a button that says "Add Recipe." By changing the label prop, the same MyButton component can display any text you want. Props let components be reusable and flexible.

In the Bolt workflow, you might not directly write out these props in code, but you *will* describe things that translate to props. For instance, if you tell Bolt, "Add a button that says 'Save Recipe' next to each recipe," Bolt will generate something like <Button label="Save Recipe" /> under the hood (or it might put the text directly into a standard <button> element). The key concept is *passing data into components*, which is what's happening behind the scenes whenever you specify details in your prompt.

Another way to think about props is to imagine you're ordering a custom car. You might specify the color, the engine type, the interior fabric, and so on. Those specifications are like props for the car-building process. Similarly, when you say to Bolt, "I want each recipe card to show the cooking time and difficulty level," you're essentially specifying props for the RecipeCard component. For instance, each recipe card might get a time prop and a difficulty prop to display. Bolt takes your specification and applies it to the components it creates.

State: Managing Dynamic Data and Interaction

While props are inputs to a component from the outside, *state* is a component's own internal memory. State is used for data that changes over time or in response to user actions. For example, if you have a checkbox that can be checked or unchecked, its current "checked" or "unchecked" status could be part of the application's state (because it can change when the user clicks it). If you have a list that can expand and collapse, whether it's expanded or not is part of the state.

In React, a component can have *state variables*, or variables that store information about some aspect of the state. When those state variables change, such as when you expand or collapse the list, the component automatically rerenders (updates its output) to reflect the new state. Let's look at a quick example of state in a component. Imagine a counter that increases when you click a button:

```
import { useState } from 'react';

function Counter() {

  const [count, setCount] = useState(0);


  return (

    <div>

      <p>You clicked {count} times.</p>

      <button onClick={() => setCount(count + 1)}>Click me</button>

    </div>

  );

}
```

In this `Counter` component, we use React's `useState` hook to create a state variable `count` (with an updater function called `setCount`). The count starts at 0. The component displays the current count and a button that, when clicked, increments the count. Each time you click, `setCount(count + 1)` updates the state, and React rerenders the `<p>` tag to show the new count. This all happens seamlessly, so the text "You clicked X times" updates in real time as you press the button.

Now, when you're using Bolt, you don't have to write `useState` or manage state directly. Bolt will handle that for you. But it's valuable to understand that when you ask for interactive features, the AI is using state under the hood. For example, if your prompt says, "When the user clicks the heart icon, mark the recipe as a favorite," Bolt will create some state (maybe an array of favorite recipe IDs or a Boolean flag on each recipe) and an `onClick` handler that updates that state. In your app, you'd just see that clicking the heart icon toggles its appearance (like filling in the heart to indicate it's saved) and maybe adds the recipe to a favorites list. That visible behavior is a result of state changes that trigger UI updates.

Understanding state also helps when refining your prompts. If something isn't updating in your app, it might be because the state isn't set up the way you expected. For instance, maybe the recipe list isn't refreshing after you add a new recipe. In a React app, that would typically mean that the state representing the list of recipes wasn't updated correctly. In Bolt, you could address that by prompting something like "After adding a new recipe, refresh the list so the new recipe appears." The AI would then adjust the code (perhaps making sure to update the recipe's state or refetch the list) to achieve the effect you want.

How React Fits into the Bolt Experience

By now you might be thinking: *This is interesting, but do I really need to know all this to use Bolt?* The answer is no, not in order to get started—but it will help a great deal as you build more complex apps. Knowing these React concepts can guide how you phrase your prompts and how you interpret Bolt's outputs.

For example, if you understand components, you might realize that a big, complicated page can be broken into smaller parts. You could then prompt Bolt in steps:

> Create a header component with the app logo and navigation menu.

Then:

> Now create a main dashboard component that shows the user's stats.

Then:

> Add a footer component with contact information.

You don't have to use the word *component* in your prompt (Bolt will often figure it out), but being aware of this structure lets you think in a modular way, which often leads to clearer prompts.

Similarly, awareness of props might lead you to specify things like this:

> Show the user profile component with the user's name and profile picture.

In React terms, Bolt might have a `UserProfile` component where it passes the name and picture URL as props. If you later say, "Update the user profile to also show the user's title (like Engineer or Designer)," what you're effectively doing is asking Bolt to add another prop to that component (like `title`) and display it. Understanding that relationship can make your mental model of the app clearer.

State is perhaps the most important concept to grasp when dealing with interactivity. If you know that state is what's behind dynamic behavior, you can structure your prompts to talk about those behaviors. "When the user clicks X, do Y" is essentially you describing an event that should change some state (and thus change the UI). Bolt translates that into code. If you find that something isn't working as expected after a user interaction, you can prompt in a way that tells it to correct the state logic:

> Ensure that clicking the "Load More" button actually fetches and displays the next set of results.

React, as a framework, emphasizes a certain way of thinking in which you break the UI into a component hierarchy, thinking about what each part needs (data via props) and how it can change (state). This is often called "thinking in React." You're providing the high-level vision, and Bolt is doing the low-level React thinking for you. But the more you can align your instructions with React-like thinking, the more smoothly Bolt can turn your words into a well-structured app.

As you move into actually using Bolt in the next chapters, keep these concepts in the back of your mind. They will gradually become clearer as you see them applied in practice by the AI. And if some of it still feels abstract right now, don't worry. Bolt will provide plenty of concrete examples as it builds apps for you, and I'll continue to explain what's happening along the way.

Summary

This chapter introduced you to Bolt.new and the concept of prompt-first development, where natural language becomes your primary programming interface. Rather than writing code line by line, you can describe what you want to build and watch as AI transforms your descriptions into working applications. Bolt serves as an intelligent apprentice that handles the heavy lifting of coding while you guide the creative direction, making software development accessible to anyone who can clearly articulate their ideas.

The benefits of this approach are transformative across skill levels. For beginners, it dramatically lowers the barrier to entry, allowing you to build functional prototypes without years of programming study. Experienced developers can use it to rapidly prototype ideas and eliminate tedious setup work, focusing their expertise on complex logic and creative problem-solving. Even nontechnical professionals like designers, product managers, and entrepreneurs can create working demos to communicate their visions more effectively than any written specification could achieve.

Understanding React's core concepts—components, props, and state—will enhance your effectiveness with Bolt, even though you don't need to write React code directly. Components are the building blocks that divide your UI into manageable pieces, props are the data you pass to customize those components, and state manages the dynamic, interactive aspects of your application. When you describe features in your prompts, you're essentially specifying how these React concepts should work together, and Bolt translates your vision into properly structured code.

The iterative nature of prompt-first development encourages experimentation and refinement. Through a conversational back-and-forth with the AI, you can gradually sculpt your application into the exact form you envision. This process teaches you to think clearly about what you want to build, breaking down complex ideas into specific, actionable descriptions. As you continue your journey with Bolt, remember that success comes from clear communication, patient iteration, and understanding the underlying structure of modern web applications.

CHAPTER 2

Getting Started with Bolt

Now that we've covered the big ideas behind Bolt and some fundamentals of how web apps are structured, it's time to roll up your sleeves and actually *use* it. In this chapter, I will walk you through the Bolt interface to create your first project. By the end of this chapter, you'll have a working app (built with Bolt's help) and a solid understanding of how to navigate the Bolt workspace.

Signing Up and Launching Bolt

To get started, open your web browser and navigate to bolt.new (simply type "bolt.new" in the address bar). The site greets you with a simple question: "What do you want to build?" This is your invitation to start prompting.

Before you dive in with an answer, you should sign in or create an account, especially if you want to save your work. Bolt is built by StackBlitz, so it offers sign-in options like your GitHub account, your Google account, or an email. Choose the method you prefer and log in (see Figure 2-1).

Once signed in, you'll be taken to the Bolt development workspace (see Figure 2-2).

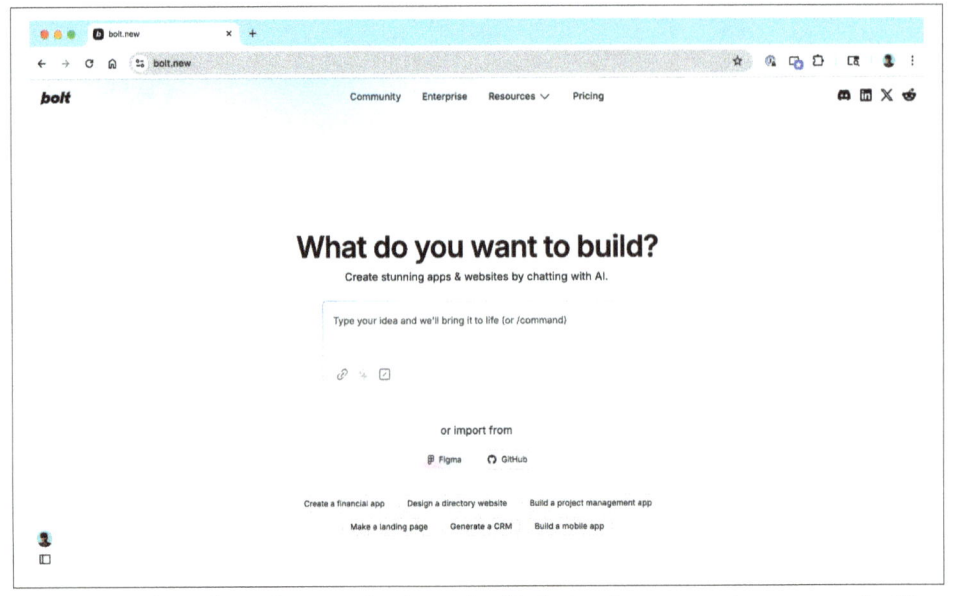

Figure 2-1. The Bolt workspace after login, highlighting the prompt input area, the file explorer, the code editor, and preview sections

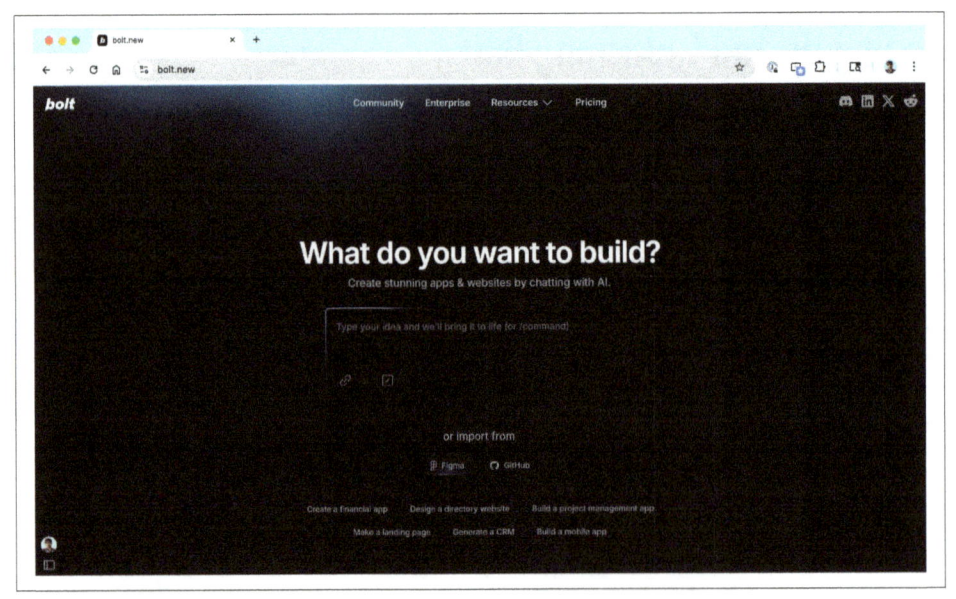

Figure 2-2. Bolt.new's prompt input field in dark mode, a visually accessible option

This is where all the magic happens. Let's familiarize you with what's on the screen. You should see a prominent area to enter your prompt (often on the side or bottom of the screen, resembling a chat interface). There will also be an editor section, where code files are displayed, and a preview area, where you'll see your running application. The exact layout might vary or evolve, but generally it includes:

Prompt input

A text box or chat window where you type instructions to Bolt. It might have placeholder text like "How can Bolt help you today?" This is where you'll converse with the AI.

File explorer

A panel listing the files and folders of your project (usually on the left side). Until you give Bolt a prompt to generate something, this might be empty or show a minimal set of files.

Code editor

The main area where the content of the files is shown. You can click on a file from the explorer to view its code here. Bolt will automatically open and display files as it creates or modifies them.

Preview/output

A section or panel (often on the right side or maybe as a separate tab) where the live application runs. This is essentially a mini web browser inside Bolt that shows your app in action, updating as changes are made. You saw this in Figures 1-1 and 1-2 in Chapter 1.

Control bar

At the top of the workspace, you might find buttons and indicators (Figure 2-3). Common ones include Deploy, Download, Open in StackBlitz, and possibly Clear or New to start fresh. There may also be a token-usage indicator or settings icon.

Don't worry if your interface looks slightly different or if new features have been added. Bolt is evolving, but the core idea remains: you have a chat-based interface you can use to talk to the AI and a real development environment to see and edit what it builds.

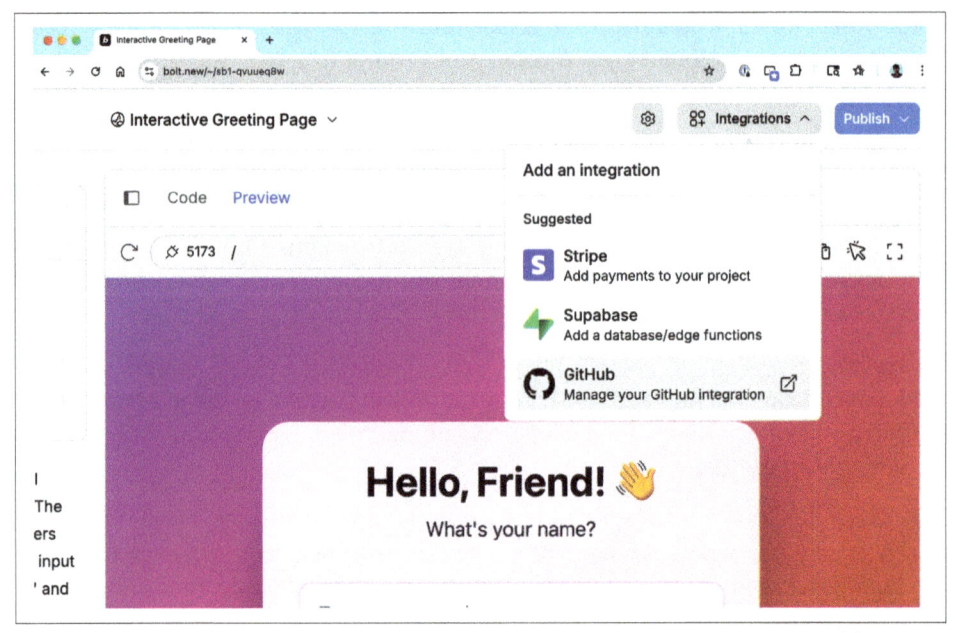

Figure 2-3. Bolt's interface lets you toggle between Code and Preview views, add an integration, or Publish (deploy) the app to the web

Your First Prompt

Let's build something! For your very first project in Bolt, we'll start simple, since we want this to be accessible even if you have minimal coding experience. Let's try a friendly greeting app that greets the user by name. It's simple, but it touches on both input (the user can type their name) and output (the app responds with a greeting), which makes it a great place to start.

In the prompt input area, type something like this (you can phrase it in your own words, of course):

> Create a simple web page that greets the user. It should have a text input where the user can type their name, and a heading that says "Hello, [Name]!" which updates as the name is typed. Make the design friendly and colorful.

Now, take a deep breath and hit Enter (or click the Send button if there is one). This is the moment of truth—you're giving instructions to Bolt, and the AI is about to work its magic. Behind the scenes, Bolt is interpreting your prompt. It understands that you want an input box for the name and a heading that changes to greet the user by name. It also caught the part about a friendly, colorful design, which means it might choose a cheerful color scheme or font.

Within a few seconds, you should see Bolt responding in the chat. It might say something along the lines of this:

> Sure, I'll create a greeting app with an input and dynamic heading. I'll set up a React project and add the requested features.

The exact wording can vary, but Bolt typically confirms what it understood and outlines the steps it will take. This gives you insight into what the AI is doing. For instance, if it mentions React (as in this example), you now know the underlying tech it's using for the frontend.

There is a small possibility that a problem may occur during code generation. In such cases, Bolt will often alert you to these errors ("Potential problems detected") and may even make an attempt to fix these for you: "I can see the issue clearly. I'll fix this by…"

 AI is *nondeterministic*, which means that you can get different results even if you use the same prompt. When you see me refer to what Bolt "might" do or "will probably" do, that's because your results may vary. However, while it might make different choices, the general behavior you can expect should be the same as, or very close to, what I describe in the text. When I don't use these "hedge" terms, you can assume that they're implied.

The first prompt might take half a minute or so because Bolt is setting up an entire project, but you will see the results shortly. The file explorer will populate with a bunch of files: probably things like *index.html*, some source-code files (maybe *App.jsx* or *index.js*, depending on the stack), possibly a *package.json* listing dependencies, and so on. Bolt has effectively created a new project for you. In the code editor, Bolt often opens a file it wants to show you—likely the main file of the app—with the code it wrote. In the preview panel, you should now see your app in action, as shown in Figure 2-4.

Try it out! In the preview, there should be an input box. Click it and type your name. If you type "Jane," you should see the heading change in real time. It's possible Bolt and its underlying models may try to add additional UX features to your app that were not in the original prompt if it believes they will be useful. By the time you've typed the whole name, the page will display "Hello, Jane!" in a friendly style.

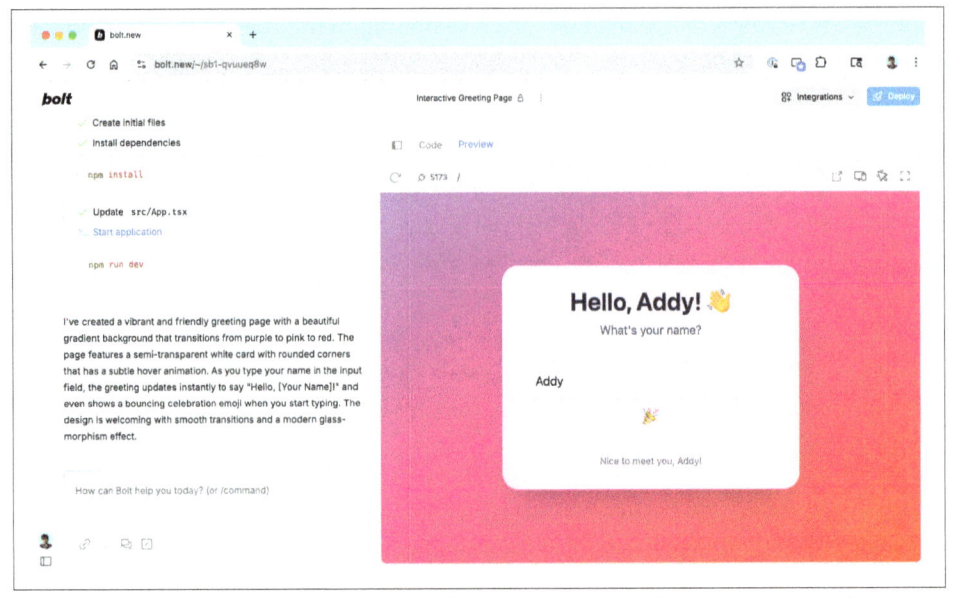

Figure 2-4. The greeting app running in the Bolt preview, with a text input and a "Hello, Name!" message visible

Take a moment to appreciate what just happened. You just described an app in English, and Bolt built it and ran it for you. How cool is that?

Navigate to the code editor and scroll through the code Bolt wrote (Figure 2-5). You might see that it created an App component with a bit of state to hold the current input value (the name) and an `<input>` field with an event handler, so it can update the greeting as you type. It also likely added some CSS or styling directly to make the page colorful, as requested. Even if you don't understand the code fully, you can glean some information from reading it. Notice that the structure of the code reflects what you asked for: there's an input element and a display of the greeting text.

This is a simple app, but you've successfully gone through the core workflow: prompt → generate → view → interact. You communicated your idea, Bolt implemented it, and you got to see and use the result immediately. For a beginner, this is a huge leap: you bypassed a lot of the setup and syntax hurdles that you'd normally encounter.

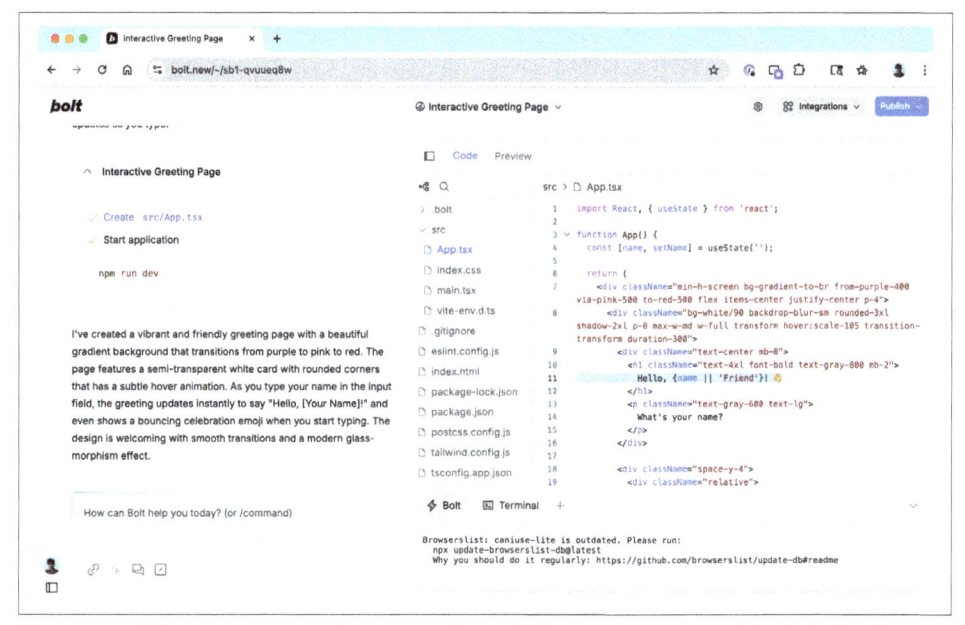

Figure 2-5. The autogenerated source code and file structure created by Bolt for the recipe app

Navigating and Tweaking the Workspace

Now that your app is running, let's look around the Bolt interface a bit more. On the left, in the file explorer, you can click on different files. For example, you might find a file that contains the text "Hello, …" This is likely where the greeting is rendered. If you click it, the code editor will show you that code. You can edit this code manually if you want to experiment. For instance, you could change the default greeting or styling. If you do, you'll typically see the changes reflected in the preview. Bolt may autorestart the dev server, or you might have to refresh to see changes if it doesn't happen automatically.

Let's identify some key controls in the interface:

Chat panel

This is where your conversation with Bolt lives. You should see your initial prompt and Bolt's reply. You can scroll up to review them. If Bolt's response was long or if it wrote a lot of code, it might summarize and not show all of the code in chat (since the code is in the editor). But it might indicate what files it created or changed. The chat panel is also where you'll type follow-up prompts (more on that in the next chapter, when you refine your app).

Clear/Reset

If you see a button labeled Clear or New Project, that's what you can use to start over from scratch. Using it will wipe the current chat and project away, giving you a fresh slate. Use it only when you want to abandon the current project, because once you clear, you'll lose the current conversation context in the chat. (If you saved or downloaded your code, the code remains saved externally; if you didn't, it's gone.) If something goes really off track, clearing is a way to begin anew.

Download

Look for a Download icon or button. Clicking this will let you save your project's code as a ZIP file to your computer. This is great if you want to keep a copy of the code, share it manually, or open it later in your own IDE.

Open in StackBlitz

StackBlitz is the underlying platform that Bolt is built on. When you click "Open in StackBlitz," your project will load in a more traditional editor view on stackblitz.com. This is useful if you want to switch to a manual coding mode or explore the project's structure in depth. In StackBlitz, you won't have the AI chat, but you can edit and run the code and even commit it to a GitHub repository if you wish.

Deploy

When you click Deploy, Bolt will bundle your application and host it online. By default, Bolt uses a service called Netlify to deploy. After a short build process, you'll get a public URL, something like *https://friendly-greeting-12345.netlify.app* (this URL won't work; the exact URL is usually a unique combination of words and numbers). This is a live version of your app on the internet! You can send your URL to a friend, and they'll see the greeting app you just made.

Settings/Account

There will be a settings menu (under a gear icon). Here you can find things like your token usage (Bolt has a generous limit on free AI tokens per day), subscription options if you need more tokens, backup management (we'll talk about backups in Chapter 4), and other advanced features. In this context, *tokens* are the fundamental units of text that the AI model uses to process information. When you interact with Bolt, you consume these tokens in various ways, including during chat interactions, code generation, and when the AI analyzes existing code. You'll also find a link to the Bolt.new help center in the sidebar, which can be handy if you forget where a feature is.

Understanding Metaprompts: Your Project's AI Guide

Bolt uses metaprompts—also known as system or project prompts—to guide its AI engine's behavior and context. You can customize them so Bolt follows your high-level style, architecture, or guidelines across a project.

If you scan through your project files, you may also notice a special file labeled simply `prompt` under the Bolt directory (see Figure 2-6). This file contains your project metaprompt and acts like a mission statement for the assistant—guiding it to follow a consistent set of principles throughout your app.

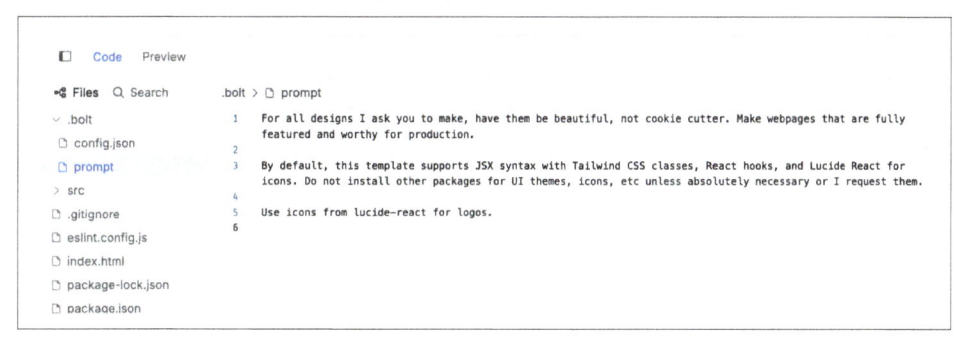

Figure 2-6. System prompt in Bolt

For example, it might contain something like this:

> For all designs I ask you to make, have them be beautiful, not cookie cutter. Make web pages that are fully featured and worthy for production.
>
> By default, this template supports JSX syntax with Tailwind CSS classes, React hooks, and Lucide React for icons. Do not install other packages for UI themes, icons, etc., unless absolutely necessary or I request them.
>
> Use Icons from lucide-react for logos.

Let's consider how Bolt uses metaprompts (Figure 2-7).

A *global system prompt* is applied across all projects and prompts unless you override it. It defines a consistent style or constraints for your work. For example:

> Always use functional React components with Tailwind CSS.

A *project prompt* is specific to the current project you're working on. Project prompts are perfect for rules like these:

> Only modify [file X] when changing styles.
>
> Use Expo and React Navigation structure.

You can set a project or global prompt by navigating to Settings → Knowledge in Bolt's sidebar. You'll see fields for Project Prompt and Global System Prompt. Edit them to add your rules and click Save. Every new prompt you enter will now be prefaced with these instructions.

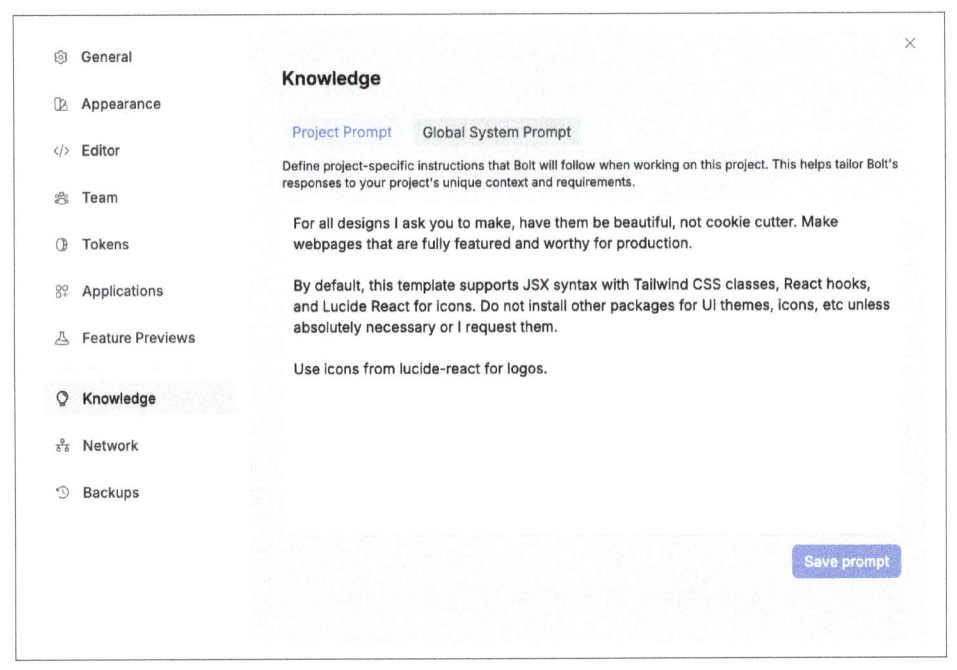

Figure 2-7. Changing the system prompt in Bolt

So why do metaprompts matter? They enforce consistency, making sure Bolt always respects the formatting, architecture, or design choices you prefer. They're also efficient, cutting down on the need to repeat instructions ("don't touch this file," "use X library"). Using them also helps reduce errors, like the AI modifying the wrong files or introducing unwanted dependencies.

Example: Metaprompting

Let's say that you want Bolt to always prefer TypeScript for all files and code snippets. You decide to put this preference in a project prompt:

> Prefer TypeScript for all files and code snippets. When adding components or utilities, follow idiomatic TypeScript patterns with clear types and interfaces.

Every time you ask Bolt to do something like "add a settings screen," it will honor these constraints as part of its system-level context—so you don't have to repeat them.

Summary

You have successfully created a project on Bolt. You've logged in, entered a prompt, witnessed the AI at work, and seen your app run. You've also learned where to find the essential tools in the interface—and how metaprompts shape your entire project.

Before moving on, take some time to play around if you want. Maybe change the prompt slightly and run it again, or try a different small idea. The more you explore, the more comfortable you'll become. Just remember, if you start a new idea, use the Clear/New button so you don't confuse Bolt with context from the previous app. Each project you build in Bolt is kept separate in its chat history.

In the next chapter, we'll get into the real heart of developing with Bolt: mastering the art of prompts and steering the AI to get exactly what you want. You'll use what you've built here as a starting point. I'll show you how to refine it, plus we'll try out other kinds of applications. So far, you've seen the basics of how to start a project—now it's time to become a prompt artisan and unlock Bolt's full potential.

CHAPTER 3

Be Clear, Be Specific: Prompt Engineering and Iterative Development

Now that you've seen an app come to life from a single prompt, it's time to dive deep into the art and science of writing prompts. This chapter will show you how to get the best results and how to manage the output the AI gives you. Think of this as learning to communicate with your apprentice—they're extremely smart, fast, and knowledgeable, but they need clear instructions and a bit of guidance.

I'll cover techniques for crafting good prompts, refining your app's behavior and design through natural language, and handling the AI's responses (including when it doesn't do exactly what you want), and I'll show you some best practices for a smooth prompt-first workflow. By the end of this chapter, you should feel confident in explaining what you want (even if you don't know how to code it yourself) and directing Bolt to build it.

Managing Expectations: AI's Limitations and Strengths

As you continue to work with Bolt, it's important to maintain realistic expectations and leverage the AI's strengths. Bolt is incredibly powerful at generating code quickly and following instructions, but it's not infallible or all-knowing. It can't instantly create a perfect, production-ready app without your input and guidance. Sometimes it will make an assumption that you didn't intend, and it won't know what's on your mind unless you tell it explicitly.

One limitation to be aware of is the AI's memory, or *context window*. Like other AI assistants based on LLMs, Bolt has a limit to how much conversation history and code it can pay attention to at once. If your project becomes very large or your chat very long, Bolt might start forgetting or ignoring details you gave it earlier. If you notice this, the remedy is usually to gently remind it in your prompt. There's no harm in restating your requirements:

> Just to recap, we have tasks with projects and a dashboard. Now I want to add...

This way, you're bringing the important context back to the forefront.

Bolt's strength is generating boilerplate and hooking things up quickly, but it might not always pick the optimal solution or design pattern the way a seasoned human developer would. That's OK for many cases, especially prototypes. If you have some coding knowledge, you can always instruct it to use a different library or structure. If you don't, you still have a working app. Just be mindful that not all AI-generated code follows best practices, especially for code that's intended for production. However, for learning and quick building, it's usually more than sufficient.

Sometimes Bolt does what you ask but overlooks a detail or two. Always verify by testing the app's behavior, and identify any gaps between what you imagined and what Bolt delivered.

On the flip side, an AI's strength is that it's tireless and not easily frustrated by changes or repetitive tasks. You can ask Bolt to do something 10 times in slightly different ways and it won't complain. This invites experimentation. If a design isn't clicking for you, try describing it differently or ask for alternatives:

> Give the app a different theme—maybe try a dark theme with gold accents.

You can even ask Bolt for suggestions. It might come up with an idea you hadn't thought of.

When you're not sure how to phrase your instructions, Bolt's interface includes a little sparkle icon or something similar next to the prompt input. This is the "Enhance prompt" feature, and when you click it, the AI model will rewrite or expand your prompt for clarity. Essentially, it helps you prompt-engineer on the fly. "Enhance prompt" is especially useful when you're not sure what details the AI needs. Bolt has context about what's already in your project, so it can infuse the prompt with specifics.

For instance, you might type "Add a dark-mode toggle" then hit Enhance. Bolt might transform that into a more detailed prompt like this:

> Implement a dark mode toggle in the top-right of the navbar. Use a sun/moon icon to indicate the mode, and persist the user's theme choice (e.g., using localStorage).

You can review this suggestion, tweak if needed, and send it, or just use it as a guide for your own phrasing.

Effective Prompting Tips

A good prompt is just a good set of instructions. The more unambiguous and clear it is, the more likely you are to get the outcome you expect. That said, you don't always have to spell out every tiny detail. Bolt is trained to fill in reasonable defaults. Whenever you have a strong idea about something, though, say it.

Here are some guidelines for writing effective prompts:

Describe features and behavior
Focus on what you want the app to do. For example, if it's a fitness tracker, list the key features:

> Allow users to log workouts by type (running, weightlifting, etc.), track progress over time, and display a summary dashboard with charts.

If it's an ecommerce frontend, enumerate what it should have:

> Create a product listing page with images, a product detail page, a shopping cart, and a checkout form.

Mention the context or purpose
Sometimes explaining the purpose helps the AI make design decisions. Saying "a to-do app for managing daily tasks" versus "a project management app for team collaboration" could lead Bolt to different interpretations (the latter might include user accounts or sharing features). So give a one-line context if relevant: "for a team," "for personal use," "for kids," and so on.

Specify the look and feel
This is where you convey the vibe. Adjectives and analogies are your friends here. You can say things like "with a modern look and feel," "like a professional dashboard you'd see in a finance app," "with playful, cartoon-style graphics and vibrant colors," or "in the style of a social media feed." Don't worry if you're not a designer—just describe the impression you want the app to give. For example, "a cozy, warm design like a coffee shop ambiance" could translate to a brown and beige color scheme with cursive fonts, whereas "sleek and techy" might result in dark backgrounds and neon accents.

Name important technologies (if you know them)
Bolt can work with many frameworks and libraries. If you have a particular one in mind, mention it early: "Build a blog site using Next.js" or "Create a landing page using plain HTML/CSS with no frameworks." If you don't mention any technologies, Bolt will choose a default (often React with a simple setup). If you don't know or don't care about this, it's fine to omit it—Bolt will make a reasonable choice for you.

Use cue phrases to keep prompts manageable

If you have a laundry list of features, don't dump them all in one giant paragraph at the start. Break it down. It's OK to say, "First, set up the basic app with user login and a home page. We'll add more features next." The phrase "we'll add more features next" clues in Bolt that this is an iterative process: after the first part is done, you'll tackle the next set of features. This helps avoid confusion and makes it easier to pinpoint issues if something goes wrong.

Ask for help or examples

If you're unsure how to phrase something, you can ask Bolt for guidance:

> I want to add a feature for X, but I'm not sure how to describe it well. Can you help me outline it?

Bolt is quite capable of helping you refine your request. You can use the "Enhance prompt" feature to suggest improvements to your phrasing. This can be a useful way to learn how to communicate with the AI.

You can always rephrase and try again if a prompt doesn't yield what you expect. I'll guide you through that a little later in this chapter.

Start Broad, Then Refine

One of the key strategies in prompt-first development is to begin with a broad prompt and then iteratively refine. In other words, you start by describing your app at a high level to get the basic structure in place, and then you make it better step by step. This approach works well because your first prompt, being broad, gives Bolt the freedom to scaffold the project in a reasonable way. Then you can get more specific with subsequent prompts.

Once you've seen Bolt build a basic app, you're ready to try your own variation. Let's do this for real: you'll create a personal task-manager app (essentially a to-do list with some extra features). Start with this prompt:

> Build a to-do list application where users can add tasks, mark tasks as completed, and remove tasks.

This simple prompt defines the core functionality of your app but not much else. Based on it, Bolt will set up a basic to-do app, perhaps with an input field and button to add tasks, a list display, and a way to check off or delete tasks. The design might be plain, but that's OK for a first iteration.

Once you see the basic app working, it's time to add details and improvements. You could follow up with this:

> Make the app use a modern, minimalist design with a soft color palette, and add a feature to edit existing tasks.

Here, you're addressing two aspects: the visual style ("modern, minimalist design, soft colors") and functionality (adding the edit feature for tasks). Bolt will take this and apply changes: perhaps it will update the CSS to use a nicer font and colors, add an edit button next to each task, and implement the logic to update a task's text.

Notice what you just did: you gave it the big picture first and the details after. You could have tried to cram everything into one prompt:

> Build me a to-do app with add, complete, delete, edit features, with a modern minimalist design, soft colors, using a funky font, and also make it sync to local storage.

Bolt might handle it, but there's a risk it could miss something or get overwhelmed. By splitting the task into steps, you give yourself the chance to check each piece.

This leads to an important tip: *don't hesitate to iterate*. After Bolt gives you an app, evaluate it and decide on next steps. Think of each prompt as an iteration. After each step, try the app, review what was generated, and consider what you want to improve next. This might involve adding new features, tweaking the design, or fixing parts that don't quite match your vision. Then formulate your next prompt to address those points. Real development—prompt-first or otherwise—is an iterative process.

When iterating, a good mindset is to change one thing at a time—or a small, logical group of related things. For instance, you might first focus on getting the core features working, then refine the visual design, or vice versa, if getting the look and feel right is more important to you early on. If you're ever unsure, lean toward smaller steps. It gives you more control and makes it easier to understand what changed and why.

Step by Step, Task by Task

If you're building something complex, you can tackle it feature by feature. Say you want to expand that to-do app into a more full-featured task manager gradually. Your first prompt makes a basic to-do list. Your second prompt edits and improves the design. The third prompt could be:

> Allow tasks to be categorized by project. Users should be able to switch between projects (like tabs or a drop-down to select the current project) and see separate task lists for each.

That's a bigger new feature. Bolt will likely need to adjust the data structures (maybe using an array of projects, each with its own tasks) and update the UI (adding a project selector). You gave all this as one request, which is OK because it's a contained concept (projects for tasks). After it does that, you can test it. Depending on how it goes, your next iteration might be polishing the design or adding another feature:

> Add a search bar to filter tasks.

At each step, test the app as thoroughly as you can. Click every button; try edge cases. If you find a problem, like something that doesn't work on the second try or a layout that breaks on mobile, bring that up with Bolt:

> The layout looks weird on my phone screen—the sidebar overlaps the task list. Make it responsive: on small screens, put the sidebar as a top menu instead of on the side.

A prompt like this points out a specific issue (the sidebar overlapping) and gives a direction for the solution (rearrange the layout on small screens). Bolt can then modify the CSS or layout code accordingly. This way, you guide the app toward robustness.

Remember, Bolt's ability to run the app instantly means you get *continuous feedback*, and you should take advantage of that. This is similar to traditional development best practices, which include running and testing your code frequently. Here, you're writing in natural language and the AI is doing the code changes, but you, as the developer, still need to verify that the changes accomplish what you want.

While iterating, keep notes of what you've already changed and what changes are still pending. Bolt remembers the entire project it has built so far (within the limits of its memory, known as the *context window*), so you can refer back to previous decisions in your prompts:

> Earlier we made the dashboard with a pie chart, but now I realize I want it to be a bar chart instead.

You can say that directly, and Bolt will replace the pie with a bar chart. It's aware of what "the dashboard" is because it built that dashboard just a few prompts ago (assuming you're within the context window size). If you're not sure Bolt remembers a detail in a long conversation, it's never a bad idea to reiterate it in another prompt. Usually, though, referring to a component by name (like "the dashboard" or "the tasks list") is enough for the AI to latch onto the relevant part of the project.

"Vibe Coding" and Creative Exploration

Earlier, I mentioned the term *vibe coding*. This is a playful term the software development community uses to describe coding by feel, focusing on the experience and atmosphere of the app rather than detailed specifications. Bolt is a perfect tool for vibe coding because, when you describe the *feeling* you want, it will try to manifest that feeling in the app's design and behavior.

Let's say you want to create a small web app for a local bakery to display their menu and daily specials. You might not know anything about web development or design, but you have a vibe in mind: you want it to feel warm and welcoming, just like the bakery, with maybe a touch of vintage style. You could prompt:

> Build a simple website for a bakery that shows today's specials and a menu. It should feel warm and welcoming, with a bit of a vintage cafe style (think rustic and cozy). Use colors and fonts that match that vibe.

This prompt is driven largely by the feeling, and you leave a lot of the specifics to the AI (like exactly how the specials are shown or what the layout is). Bolt would then generate an app that likely has a homey style: perhaps a warm color scheme of browns or pastel oranges, an elegant cursive font for headings, and some images of baked goods if available. Functionally, it will include sections for specials and the menu.

The beauty of vibe coding is that it encourages creativity and rapid prototyping. You can throw an idea at Bolt and see what comes out. Maybe you want to experiment with different styles:

> Now make it a modern style with bold, clean lines and a dark background.

With one prompt, the bakery site could transform into something entirely different visually. This is like having a design assistant along with a coding assistant.

For nontechnical builders or developers ideating, vibe coding lowers the pressure of "getting it right" in terms of technical details. You can iteratively converge on something cool. Perhaps you start with this:

> I want a fun app for tracking daily moods, kind of like a Tamagotchi pet that reflects how I'm feeling.

You might not even know where to begin implementing that traditionally, but Bolt might create a cute character whose expression changes based on input mood, etc. Then you refine:

> Make the character bigger and animate it when the mood is updated.

Each change is guided by the vibe you want (fun, interactive, playful).

Keep in mind, vibe coding doesn't mean you ignore functionality. It's more about an approach: you let the details emerge through iteration, guided by how each version "feels" to you. With Bolt, because trying a change is as easy as describing it and pressing Enter, you can afford to try lots of small tweaks. You become a kind of *experience DJ*, mixing visuals and features by ear (or rather, by eye) to see what looks and feels right.

Guiding Bolt When Things Go Off Track

Working with AI means sometimes you'll get output that isn't what you had in mind. Maybe the feature works but the UI isn't where you wanted it, or the AI misunderstood your instructions and built something slightly different. When that happens, don't panic. There are ways to steer Bolt back on course.

The first tool is, of course, your next prompt. Address the issue directly. Suppose you ask for a "dashboard with charts," and Bolt gives you a table of numbers but no charts. You can follow up with this:

> I actually wanted graphical charts (like bar or line charts) on the dashboard. Please add a bar chart showing X and a line chart showing Y.

Being direct like this is usually enough. Bolt will recognize that it missed the mark and then incorporate a chart library or some visualization to satisfy your request.

Sometimes Bolt might partially implement something or make a decision you didn't expect. For example, maybe it adds a login system when you didn't ask for one, or it uses a layout that you find odd. Feel free to tell Bolt:

> Remove the login requirement; the app should not ask for users to sign in.

Or:

> The layout is a single column, but I'd prefer a two-column layout with the menu on the left and content on the right.

You're the director here; the AI is the crew. If the set needs rearranging, just say so.

An advanced way to guide Bolt's focus is to tell it exactly which part of the app to work on:

> In the task list component, change the edit functionality to use an inline input field instead of a pop-up.

By naming "the task list component," you're signaling to Bolt to focus its changes there. If you know the file name or component name (maybe by looking at the code), you can mention it directly: "Update *TaskList.jsx* so that..." Bolt will then target its modifications to that file. You can also use the Bolt interface's feature to "target" a file by right-clicking that file. This makes the AI pay attention only to that file for the next prompt. These targeted approaches ensure you don't get unintended side effects elsewhere in the app when you make a specific change.

Bolt also provides the ability to lock files. If you have perfected certain files or sections of the app and you don't want Bolt to inadvertently mess them up while responding to a prompt, you can lock them. Similarly, targeting specific files for changes helps avoid collateral edits. These features put you in control of how broad or narrow Bolt's changes are.

Another scenario: what if Bolt does something completely off, like introducing a bug or error? For instance, you ask it to add a new feature and now the app crashes, or a button that used to work doesn't respond. This is the moment to leverage Bolt as a debugging assistant. You might say:

After you added that feature, the app began crashing when I try to add a new task. Please debug and fix the error.

Bolt can analyze its own code, often identifying the mistake (maybe it forgot to initialize something, or there's a typo) and then fixing it.

In some cases, Bolt's response might be correct but too verbose or too succinct in the UI. For example, maybe it gives users a very technical error message that's for developers. You can refine that too:

Change the error message to a simple, user-friendly text: "Oops, something went wrong. Please try again."

The AI will change the wording accordingly. Remember, you can use prompts to adjust anything about the app's behavior or content, from the placement of a button to the text on the screen.

The key to guiding Bolt is to view the AI as cooperative and amendable. It's not stubborn; it will follow your lead. So don't be shy about pointing out what's wrong and what you'd prefer. Be polite (for your own habit-building, not because the AI needs it) and be clear. You're effectively teaching it what your vision is, one prompt at a time.

Sample Prompt Scenarios

To solidify these ideas, let's look at a variety of example prompts for different kinds of apps. Each of these examples is written as a one-paragraph prompt someone might give to Bolt, along with a brief note on what the prompt is achieving. These are not exhaustive instructions, just illustrative starting points that demonstrate how you can phrase requests for different projects:

To-do list app

I want to create a simple to-do list application. Users should be able to add new tasks, mark tasks as completed, and remove tasks. The interface should be clean and minimal, with a header that says "My Tasks," an input field for adding tasks, and a list below showing all the tasks. Completed tasks should appear crossed out or greyed out.

This prompt lays out basic functionality (add, complete, remove tasks) and also gives a hint of UI (clean and minimal, with specific UI elements mentioned). Bolt will respond by setting up a straightforward to-do app following these guidelines.

Fitness tracker

Build a fitness tracker app that allows users to log their workouts. It should have a form to input a workout (type of exercise, duration, and maybe calories burned) and save it to a list of past workouts. Include a friendly dashboard that shows a summary, like total workouts this week and maybe a simple bar chart of daily exercise time. The design should be energetic and motivating, perhaps using bold colors and clear typography.

In this prompt, the features are logging workouts and seeing a summary dashboard, and the style cue is "energetic and motivating." Bolt might create a form and a list and integrate a simple chart library for the bar chart, with a bright, sporty look (Figure 3-1).

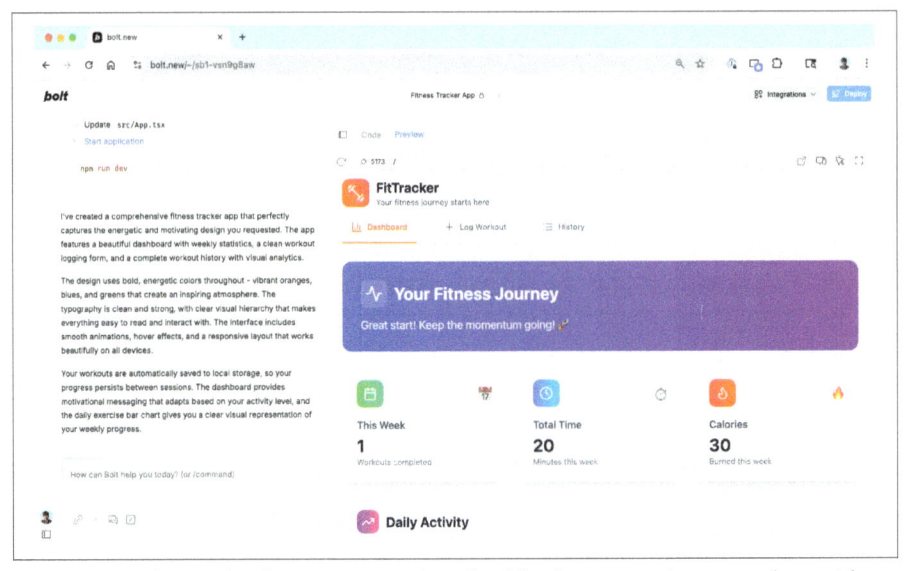

Figure 3-1. The result of prompting Bolt to build a fitness tracker, complete with dashboard stats and a colorful visual design

Ecommerce frontend

Create a frontend for an online store. Show a grid of products (each with an image, name, price, and an "Add to Cart" button). There should be a cart icon or sidebar that updates with items when they are added. Include a product detail view that pops up or goes to a new page when a product is clicked, showing a larger image and description. The style should be sleek and modern, like a tech gadget website.

This prompt is more complex. It describes multiple components (product grid, cart, detail view) and a particular interactive behavior (updating a cart). It also sets a design direction (sleek, modern, like a tech site). Bolt would likely scaffold a multipage or multicomponent app, possibly using a React state or context to handle the cart, and apply a modern UI framework or styles.

Data dashboard

> Build a dashboard for sales data. It should have a top bar with filters (like date range and product category), and below that a set of visualizations: one line chart showing sales over time, one pie chart showing sales by category, and a table listing the latest orders. Use a professional look (think corporate dashboard), with a responsive layout that works on large screens.

Here, you're asking for a data-heavy interface: filters, charts, a table. The prompt specifies exactly what charts and which table to include, and hints at responsiveness and a professional style. Bolt will probably use chart libraries like Chart.js to produce the line and pie chart, set up state for filters (maybe using sample data if it isn't connected to real data), and style it with a dark or neutral theme for that corporate feel.

Personal blog

> Generate a personal blog website. It should have a home page that displays a list of blog post titles with excerpts, a sidebar with my profile picture and a short bio, and a way to navigate to individual blog posts. The post page should show the title, date, and full content of the post, with a comments section at the bottom (just a placeholder, not functional). Use a clean, readable design—maybe similar to a Medium article layout, with plenty of white space and a serif font for the text.

This prompt outlines a content-driven site with multiple pages (home and post pages). It asks for design inspiration from Medium.com (clean, readable, serif font). Bolt would likely create a routing structure for pages and sample posts data, and it would style the typography nicely, giving an elegant blog feel.

Each of these examples demonstrates a mix of describing functionality and describing the desired feel or style. You can see that none of them require mentioning actual code or implementation details, like "make an array for this" or "use a flexbox layout here"—those things are left to Bolt. Your job is to articulate what you want and, sometimes, how it should feel or look. The more practice you get, the more you'll develop an intuition for what information to include in a prompt and what to leave open-ended for the AI to decide.

Best Practices for a Prompt-First Workflow

Let's recap and highlight some best practices to make your prompt-first development smooth:

Develop incrementally

Build your app layer by layer. Start with core features, then add enhancements. Test at each step. This not only helps Bolt focus but also helps you catch issues early.

Communicate clearly

Be as clear as possible in your instructions. If something is crucial to you (like "the app must work offline" or "use my company's brand colors"), mention it. The AI can't guess your unstated preferences.

Embrace the conversation

Think of each prompt and response as a dialogue. If Bolt's output isn't exactly right, treat it as if your apprentice just gave you a draft: explain what to change and why, using the next prompt to iterate.

Use the tools provided

Make use of Bolt's interface tools. The "Enhance prompt" feature can help refine instructions. The ability to download the code or open it in StackBlitz lets you inspect or manually adjust things if needed. Targeting files or locking them to prevent changes in parts of the code can be useful for more advanced control as you become comfortable (I discuss this in more detail in Chapter 10).

Keep the user in mind

While working with AI, it's easy to get caught up in the process and forget the end user. Continuously ask yourself: Is this feature working for the user? Is the interface intuitive? If you see potential UX issues, address them in prompts:

> The user might not realize they need to click here. Add a tooltip or label to clarify.

This keeps your AI-built app user-centric.

Learn from Bolt

If you're not an expert programmer (or even if you are), take the opportunity to learn from what Bolt produces. After each major prompt, look at some of the code. See how the AI structured the app's components or how it implemented that login system you asked for. You might discover common patterns or practices. It's like reading example code for a project, except that it's written for your specific requirements.

Don't fear mistakes

Sometimes Bolt breaks something that was working (it shouldn't, but this can happen). Or you might realize halfway through that you want a different approach. It's OK. You can always ask Bolt to fix errors or, as a last resort, use the rollback feature to go back to a previous state (I'll cover that in Chapter 4). Treat it all as part of the iterative journey. One advantage of this AI-driven approach is that starting over or redoing a part of your app is relatively fast compared to writing all the code by hand.

By following these practices, you'll develop a workflow that taps into Bolt's strengths (speed, knowledge, flexibility) while mitigating its weaknesses (lack of context persistence over very long sessions; a need for explicit direction). Prompt-first development is a partnership between you and the AI, and like any partnership, good communication is key. As you gain experience, you'll start to pick up a knack for phrasing and pacing your prompts to get the best results.

The next chapter focuses on what happens when you need to make bigger changes, fix issues, or manage the history of your project. Specifically, I'll dive into Bolt's features for fixes, checkpoints, and rollbacks, which are invaluable for iterative development and maintaining control over your project as it grows.

For now, you should already feel empowered to create and refine with prompts. With practice, prompting will become second nature, and you'll be able to translate your ideas into apps with unprecedented ease.

Summary

This chapter equipped you with the essential skills for effective prompt engineering and iterative development with Bolt. The key to success lies in clear communication and managing your expectations—understanding that AI is incredibly powerful at generating code quickly but requires explicit guidance and benefits from an incremental approach. By starting with broad prompts that establish the foundation of your app and then refining through specific follow-up instructions, you can systematically build complex applications while maintaining control over the process.

The art of prompting involves balancing specificity with creative freedom. When describing your vision, focus on what the app should do rather than how it should be implemented, include contextual details about purpose and audience, and don't hesitate to use descriptive language about the look and feel you want to achieve. "Vibe coding"—building by feeling (vibes) rather than rigid specifications—becomes a powerful tool for rapid prototyping and creative exploration. Remember that each prompt is part of an ongoing conversation, and you can always correct course, address issues directly, or try different approaches without fear of permanent mistakes.

The iterative workflow is your greatest asset in prompt-first development. Test your app thoroughly after each change, tackle one feature or improvement at a time, and use Bolt's interface tools like file targeting and the "Enhance prompt" feature to maintain precision. By embracing the conversational nature of AI-assisted development and treating Bolt as a collaborative apprentice, you can rapidly transform ideas into working applications while learning from the code it generates.

CHAPTER 4

Fixes, Checkpoints, and Rollbacks

No development journey is without its detours and bumps in the road. As you build apps with Bolt, there will be times when you need to correct mistakes, improve what's already there, or even backtrack on a change that didn't work out. The good news is that Bolt provides tools to manage these situations gracefully.

In this chapter, I'll explore how to fix issues and refine your app, how to use checkpoints and rollbacks to navigate through different versions of your project, and how all this fits into an iterative development process. By understanding these features, you'll gain confidence that you can always recover from a wrong turn and continuously improve your application.

Troubleshooting

Let's face it: even with an AI helper, things can go wrong. Maybe a feature isn't working as intended, or a design change had unintended side effects. The first line of defense is to troubleshoot and fix the issue. In the previous chapter, you saw that you can directly ask Bolt to debug a problem. But let's go a bit deeper into practical troubleshooting steps in Bolt.

Suppose you notice a bug. Your app is throwing an error (you see a red error overlay in the preview or an error message in the browser console log), or perhaps nothing happens when you click a button that should do something. Here's a systematic approach:

Step 1: Identify the problem clearly
> Try to pinpoint what's not working. Maybe it's that clicking the Add to Cart button doesn't update the cart count, or the app crashes when you submit the form without filling in all of the fields. If there's an error message, note what it says. Even if it's technical gibberish to you, Bolt might understand it.

Step 2: Describe the issue to Bolt

Use a prompt to tell Bolt what's wrong and ask for a fix:

> There's a bug: when I click the "Add to Cart" button, nothing happens. Please fix it so that it adds the item to the cart and updates the cart count in the UI.

Bolt will analyze the code it wrote for that functionality and attempt a correction. Maybe a state update was missing or an event handler wasn't wired properly. Once it spots the source of the problem, it will attempt a fix and explain it in the response.

Step 3: Test the fix

Once Bolt modifies the code, try the action again. Did it solve the problem? If yes, great! If not, or if a new error arises, you can continue the conversation:

> The cart count is updating now, but it seems to always add 2 instead of 1. Please fix that logic.

This back-and-forth is very much like how you'd debug with a human partner, iteratively zeroing in on the solution.

Sometimes Bolt's changes might fix one thing but break another. For instance, in fixing the cart, maybe it accidentally breaks the remove-from-cart function. If you catch that, let Bolt know:

> Fixing the add to cart worked, but now removing an item doesn't update the count properly. Please resolve that as well.

Bolt will address it. Communicate every issue you find. The AI can't get embarrassed; it doesn't mind if you keep pointing out problems.

Another useful strategy, when you're puzzled, is to have Bolt explain the code to you:

> Explain how the cart updating logic works in this code.

Bolt can read its own generated code and tell you in plain language how it's supposed to function. This might give you insight into why a bug is happening: perhaps the cart count is being stored in one component's state but displayed from another, causing a disconnect. Once you understand the design flaw, you can direct Bolt to fix it.

It's also OK to do a little manual testing outside of Bolt's preview. For example, if the bug in question is purely visual and you suspect a CSS issue, opening the browser's developer tools in the preview frame (if accessible) might show you which element or style is problematic. For a beginner, though, stick with asking Bolt: it's simpler, and it's usually effective.

What if you ask for a complex feature and Bolt's implementation just isn't working right, even after a couple of fixes? You have a choice: you continue trying to "fix forward," moving ahead by changing the code you have, or step back and reprompt for that feature from a clean slate. This is where checkpoints and rollbacks, which we'll discuss next, come into play. One way or another, though, *any* problem in your app can be solved, either by guiding Bolt to fix it or by trying a different angle. You're never truly stuck.

Using Checkpoints and Rollbacks

Traditional software development often involves explicit version control systems (like Git) where you commit changes, branch off, etc. Bolt gives you a flavor of version control through its chat history and backup features, but without needing to know any Git commands. Each prompt is like a commit. This reinforces that development is iterative. You rarely get everything perfect in one go. Instead, you build, evaluate, tweak, maybe backtrack, then build again.

As you've seen, Bolt automatically keeps track of your project at each step of the conversation. Each prompt-and-response cycle is essentially a checkpoint in your development process. This means you can revert to an earlier state of the project if you need to.

Think of it like saving your progress in a video game. Every time you give Bolt a prompt, you're creating a new save point. If the next move doesn't work out—say, your app breaks or you don't like how something turned out—you can always reload from an earlier save and try a different path (Figure 4-1).

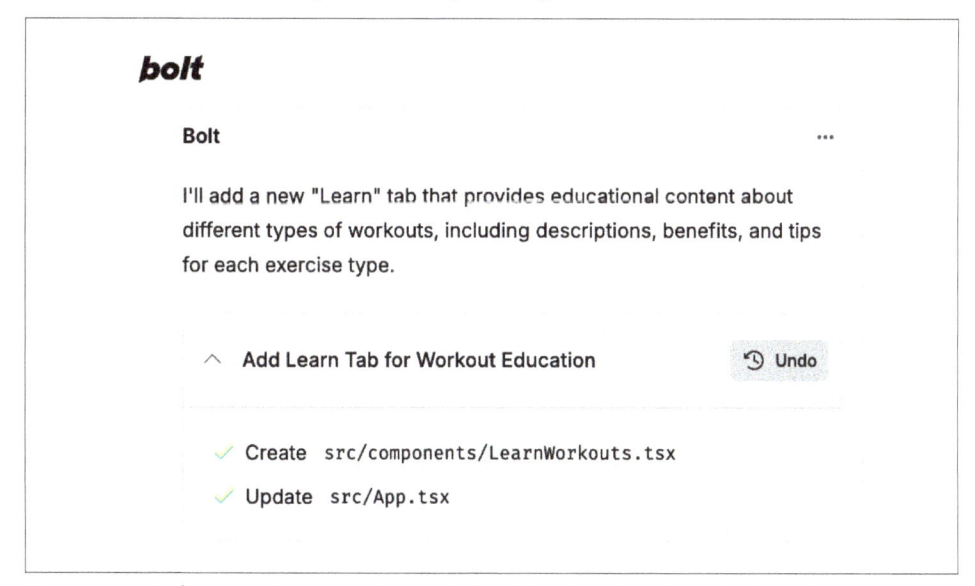

Figure 4-1. Bolt generates a new Learn Tab with educational content, and offers a one-click undo for the change

Imagine you've been working on an app for 10 prompts. Everything's been going well until prompt #11, when you ask Bolt to integrate a complex third-party API. Now the app is a mess! The layout is broken and errors are popping up. You're not sure you still want to pursue this direction.

Instead of undoing bits and pieces manually, you just revert to your last known good state—prompt #10. You've restored your app to safety. From there, you can try a different approach, ask for a simpler integration, or fix things step by step. We'll walk through how to do that next.

With a traditional coding approach, you'd likely commit your work before trying a big change—then use Git to revert if something went wrong. That works, but it requires some familiarity with version control tools.

Bolt makes this process more approachable by handling versioning automatically. Each prompt you give becomes a checkpoint you can return to. If something breaks, you can scroll back to your last stable version—say, prompt #10—and hit the Revert button in the chat interface (Figure 4-2). Confirming this (Figure 4-3) restores your project to the state it was in after that prompt, letting you safely undo the changes from prompt #11 and beyond.

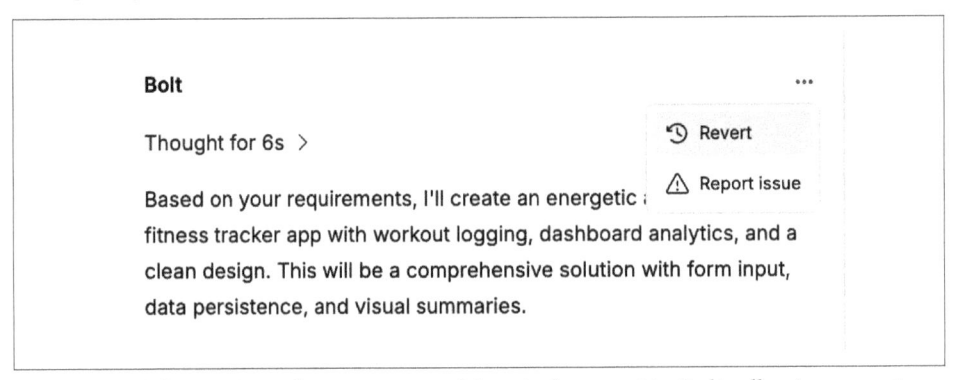

Figure 4-2. A Revert icon shown next to a historical prompt in Bolt, allowing users to go back to that app state

An effective way to use Bolt is to treat each significant prompt as a milestone. When your app reaches a working state—even if it's not complete—make a mental note: "This is a good checkpoint" (or mark the message in the interface). For example, if after prompt #8 you have a solid core app and you're about to experiment with a new feature, you know you can always roll back to that safe state if things get messy in prompts 9 through 12.

It's the safety net of version control—no setup required.

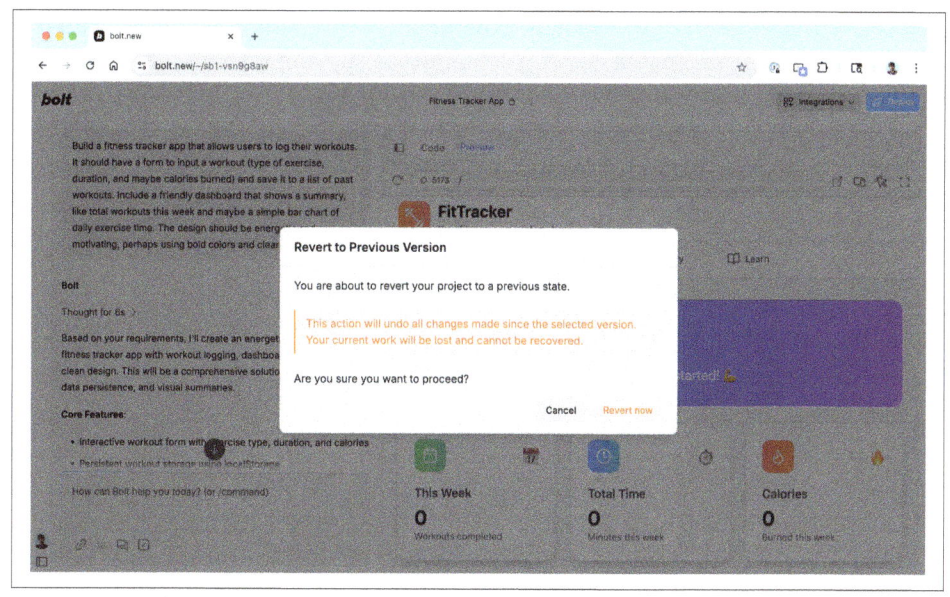

Figure 4-3. Bolt prompts you to confirm before restoring a previous project version, highlighting potential data loss

When you roll a change back, Bolt.new will typically create a new branch of the chat and start a fresh timeline from that point, often with a note like "Reverted to checkpoint from [time]." Your prompt #11 and onward from the original timeline aren't gone forever. They might still be visible above, but they are no longer the active path. This branching approach is great (and very reminiscent of Git), because you can try something else from that point without losing the option to revisit the other path if you want to.

Now, rollbacks in Bolt are not a magic undo button for everything. They reset the code to a prior state, but for your chat context, it's as if those later prompts never happened. So if you roll back and then you want to try a different approach for that feature, you'll need to provide a new prompt. For example, after rolling back the failed API integration, you might try a simpler approach—or decide to scrub the API calls for now and focus on something else.

In addition to manual rollbacks, Bolt has a backup system. It periodically saves snapshots of your project. You can also trigger backups via the interface's settings. If you go to Settings → Backups, you'll find a list of timestamps. Selecting one will open a new chat starting from that backup point. This is like branching or forking a project in Git.

Why is this useful? Perhaps you want to experiment with a radical redesign but aren't sure if you'll keep it. You could back up your current app and then, in the same chat, continue with the redesign prompts. If it goes well, great. If not, you still have the backup. You can open it separately and go right back to where you started, with no harm done. Conversely, you could open the backup first to create a new branch and do your experiments in that new branch, leaving the original project untouched.

 Before doing something major that you feel unsure about, manually create a backup. Bolt might auto-backup anyway, but doing it yourself gives peace of mind. That way, if the major change doesn't work out, you know you have a safe restore point. Going back to our game analogy, you probably want to save your game before you enter the big boss fight.

Checkpoints and rollbacks support iterative development by making it low-risk to try things. If you know that you can always roll things back, you're more likely to experiment and find the best solution. In a sense, it encourages a mindset of "move fast and don't break things (permanently)"—because you can always unbreak them by reverting.

Building Confidence by Embracing Iteration and Versioning

The true power of the prompt-first Bolt approach is that it lowers the cost of making mistakes. In software development, fear of breaking things or the effort to rewrite code can slow you down. Bolt's features like checkpoints and rollbacks, plus the ease of modifying code via prompts, means you can be bolder. Try that big redesign. Experiment with adding that complex interactive map. If it fails, you can undo it or tweak it until it works.

This iterative mindset—build, test, refine, and occasionally backtrack—is exactly how seasoned developers work too (usually with their version control systems and a lot of manual coding). You're doing the same but with an AI copilot who writes and rewrites the code for you on command.

Don't hesitate to use multiple chats or projects for different ideas. Bolt allows you to start a new project anytime, just like you did the first time. If you want to try a completely different approach or even a different app, you can do so without deleting your current one. Each chat and project is saved in your Bolt account unless you deliberately delete it. You could have one project where you experiment wildly, and another where you carefully build the polished version. The ability to copy and paste code between projects (via downloading or the editor) also means you can transfer any especially good pieces from an experiment back into your main app if needed.

Iterative development also means sometimes refactoring—restructuring the code without changing its functionality—to accommodate new needs. If your app starts simple and grows, you might find that the code needs more organization so that you can maintain it over the long term. You can ask Bolt to help with that too:

> Refactor the project to use a clearer folder structure: separate components into a components/ directory and move styles to a separate CSS file.

This kind of prompt tells Bolt to reorganize the code for maintainability. Bolt can create new files, move code around, and update references. That's something you'd do manually in a typical dev workflow, but here you can get AI assistance. Of course, always test after refactoring to ensure everything still works.

Another aspect of iteration is performance and optimization. In the early stages, you and Bolt might not worry about your app's performance—the priority is to get it working. But as you refine it, you might start noticing that, say, the app loads slowly or a certain operation is laggy. You can engage Bolt in solving that:

> The image gallery is loading very slowly. Can you optimize it? Maybe by adding lazy loading for images or optimizing image sizes.

Bolt could then implement lazy loading or suggest using a library for it. Through iterative prompts, you gradually transform a rough prototype into a more polished, efficient application. What's more, you build your confidence—you don't need to be afraid of making mistakes when you always have the option to roll them back.

When to Step In and When to Start Over

To wrap up this chapter, let's talk about two important judgment calls you'll face while working with Bolt: knowing when to step in and knowing when to start over.

When to Step In

Bolt is powerful, but it's not perfect. There will be moments when it's faster or easier to take the wheel—especially if you have some coding knowledge. For instance, if Bolt's response gets you 90% of the way there but misses a small tweak in logic, styling, or behavior, you don't have to fight with another prompt. You can jump into the code editor, make the change manually, and keep going.

Bolt supports this hybrid workflow. After a manual edit, just hit Update so that the dev server reflects your changes. Then you can continue prompting as usual—Bolt will work from the current project state, including your edits. This kind of direct intervention can help you keep momentum when prompts become less efficient than hands-on adjustment.

When to Start Over

But what if things truly go off the rails? Maybe Bolt misunderstood your prompt, or a chain of updates took the app in the wrong direction. In these cases, restarting can be a smart move.

There are a few levels to consider:

Small resets
　Ask Bolt to undo or remove the last feature. This is often enough to recover.

Rollback
　Use Bolt's rollback feature to jump back to a previous working state—like rewinding to a known good checkpoint.

Full reset
　If the project feels too tangled or messy, starting a new project from scratch is OK. You've learned from the first attempt—your next version will likely be cleaner and faster to build.

Restarting doesn't mean failure. It means you've gathered insight, and now you're ready to apply it more intentionally.

Keep Your North Star in View

Whether you're stepping in or stepping back, it helps to stay oriented toward your end goal. If you find yourself obsessing over a detail or stuck debugging, pause and ask: what are the top three things this app still needs?

Better yet, ask Bolt directly:

> Summarize the features implemented so far and identify what might be missing based on the original goal.

Bolt will give you a feature audit that helps you reset and refocus. It's a great way to regain clarity and plan your next steps with intention.

Summary

By now, you've gone from understanding what Bolt is to starting a project, mastering how to communicate with the AI, and handling the full development cycle—with all its twists and turns. You've essentially learned how to "code" by conversing. You don't need to fear complex tasks anymore. You have a copilot, a safety net, and the ability to step in—or start over—when it counts.

CHAPTER 5

Building a Movie Explorer App, Part 1: Browsing and Details

The next several chapters will walk you through five hands-on projects, demonstrating how to build and deploy applications with minimal manual coding. By the end, you'll have built several real apps, including a movie explorer, a workout tracker, and a design-driven grocery list app, by connecting Bolt with tools like the TMDB API, Netlify, Supabase, and Figma. Follow along in your browser with Bolt as you read.

In this and the next chapter, you'll build a web application we'll call Movie Explorer that allows users to browse movies and view detailed information. You'll use an API from The Movie Database (TMDB) (*https://oreil.ly/4hRZr*) to fetch data like movie titles, posters, and descriptions and display them in your app. By the end of this chapter, you'll have a functioning app where users can see popular movies, search for specific titles, and click on any movie to view its details. In Chapter 6, you'll refine the app with new features like user accounts, favorites, and more.

This chapter covers how to do the following:

- Set up a new project with Bolt
- Integrate the TMDB API by providing an API key and fetching data
- Display a list of movies (with titles and posters) on a home page
- Add a search feature to find movies by name
- Create a details page that shows more information when a movie is selected
- Do some basic UI styling for a pleasant user experience
- Test the app in the Bolt environment
- Deal with any issues (like missing data or errors)

API Key Setup

You've already set up your Bolt account, but there's one more thing you'll need before you start building: an API key (a long string of letters and numbers that authenticates your requests) to access movie data from TMDB.

If you don't have one, create a free account at *themoviedb.org*. Verify your email and log in. Navigate to your account settings and find the API section.

Follow the instructions to request an API key (for "Developer" or "Personal" use). You'll have to agree to the terms of use, and then TMDB will provide you with an API key. Treat your API key like a password, and don't share it publicly! You'll use this key in your app to fetch movie data. (For learning purposes, it's OK to embed it in our code, but for a real app, you'd keep it secret on the server.)

Setting Up a New Bolt Project

Now the fun begins. First, you need to create a new project in Bolt for your movie app. This is the same process you went through in Chapter 2, so feel free to peek back at that chapter if you need a refresher.

You'll start by telling Bolt at a high level what you want. For example, you might write something like this:

> Create a React web application called Movie Explorer that uses the TMDB API to display a list of movies. The app should have a home page showing popular movies with their titles and posters, a search bar to find movies by title, and a page to show details of a selected movie.

Let's break down what this prompt is asking for.

First, it mentions React, which you learned about in Chapter 1. Bolt supports many web frameworks, and React is a good choice for building a dynamic UI. It also gives the app a name, Movie Explorer (though you can choose any name you like). It tells Bolt to use the TMDB API. It lists some features to include: a list of movies, search, and a details page. It then broadly describes the UI as a home page with titles and posters.

When you send this prompt, Bolt will think for a moment and then start generating the project. Now, AI is *nondeterministic*, which means that you can get different results from the same prompt. Some of the details might vary a little, but I can tell you pretty confidently what Bolt will do next, which is set up a new React project structure. This should include creating files and using a framework: probably a single-page React app, since that's what the prompt specified. It will install any necessary NPM packages (like React or React Router) in the background, while the output panel tells you what it's doing. After a bit, the development server should start automatically and a preview of the app will appear.

For a prompt like "Movie Explorer" you'll typically see an app prefilled with popular movie cards, styled components, navigation, and a cinematic design theme. The generated app often includes mock data out of the box, giving you a concrete preview of how the final product could feel, rather than just an empty shell. This makes it easier to explore the structure and flow of the app right away, without having to imagine how the UI might eventually look. Figure 5-1 shows an example.

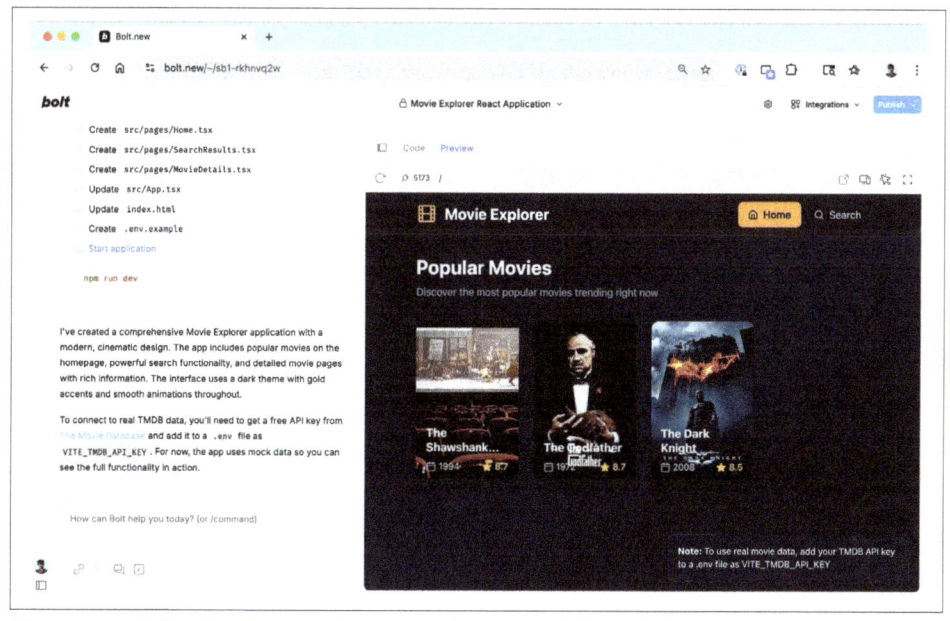

Figure 5-1. Bolt after the initial prompt, showing a fully styled Movie Explorer app with sample movie data and a note about connecting a TMDB API key

You'll also notice Bolt provides guidance on how to connect the app to real data sources. For example, a generated movie app may display sample movie listings but include a note reminding you to add your own TMDB API key in a .env file to fetch live results. The file explorer will already contain pages, components, and configuration files, giving you a functioning, styled application with basic interactivity from the start.

Configuring the TMDB API Key

Before fetching data from TMDB, you need to tell your app what the API key is. There are a couple of ways to do this. Option A is to add it to your code, which is quick and easy: you directly supply the key in a prompt, and Bolt inserts it into the code. This is *not* a best practice for real projects—it's a security risk, because it exposes the key in the code.

Option B is to use environment variables to store the key in a separate file or config that isn't exposed publicly. This is more secure. Bolt can handle this by creating an *.env* file and referencing it. However, environment variables in a frontend-only app will still get exposed when you're building, unless you use a backend proxy. For our learning purposes, we'll go with option A to avoid complexity.

> TMDB's API key is relatively low-risk because it doesn't grant access to your account, just to read data. Thus, exposing it is not catastrophic. Many client-side apps use it openly (see TMBD's Getting Started guide (*https://oreil.ly/Clw6J*)). Still, it's good to be aware that any secret you embed in frontend code can be seen by users.

For our learning purposes here, option A is the simplest way to get started. I'll show you how to secure it later, when you're deploying your app. Start with a prompt:

> Insert my TMDB API key into the project and use it for API requests. The API key is *YOUR_KEY_HERE*.

(Replace *YOUR_KEY_HERE* with your actual key string.) Bolt will update the code to include this key. It might create a variable in a config file or at the top of a file. For example, it might add a line in a config or utility file and then use this constant in fetch calls:

```
const TMDB_API_KEY = "abc123...yourkey...";
```

Or Bolt might integrate it more subtly. If Bolt asks for clarification on where to put the key, you can specify:

> Add it as a constant in the code (in a config or at top of the main file).

Fetching and Displaying Popular Movies

With our API key configured, let's get some movies! A good starting point is to have the home page display a list of popular movies when the app loads. The TMDB API has an endpoint for this: */movie/popular*. Prompt to tell Bolt exactly what you need:

> On the home page, fetch the list of popular movies from TMDB and display their poster images and titles in a grid.

Bolt will modify the home page component code. Likely actions include importing functions like `useEffect` and `useState` from React, to handle data fetching and state. Inside the home page component, Bolt will create a state variable:

```
const [movies, setMovies] = useState([])
```

It will probably use `useEffect` to fetch data when the component mounts. The fetch URL will be something like this:

```
fetch(`https://api.themoviedb.org/3/movie/popular?api_key=${TMDB_API_KEY}`)

  .then(response => response.json())

  .then(data => setMovies(data.results));
```

This calls TMDB, gets the JSON response, and updates state with the array of movies (`data.results` is an array of movie objects). Note that each movie from TMDB has a unique ID.

Next, Bolt will update the JSX to display the movies in a grid (probably using simple CSS, or maybe a framework like Bootstrap or Tailwind). The app should output an element for each movie in `movies`, possibly like this:

```
<div className="movie-card">

  <img src={/* movie poster URL */} alt={movie.title} />

  <h3>{movie.title}</h3>

</div>
```

To display the poster images, the app needs to get the correct poster URLs. TMDB gives a path. Typically, you prepend a base URL like *https://image.tmdb.org/t/p/w200* for a small image, or *w500* for something larger. Bolt might know this, since it's commonly used in examples. Ideally, it will do something like this:

```
<img src={`https://image.tmdb.org/t/p/w200${movie.poster_path}`} ... />
```

After Bolt runs this prompt, we should see the home page populate with the list of currently popular movie posters and titles.

Review the output in the app preview. You should now see multiple movie entries (Figure 5-2). They might be in a simple single column if Bolt hasn't added CSS. You asked for a grid, so Bolt might have added a CSS rule or used a flexbox or grid container. If it looks messy, with huge images or no layout, don't worry: you can fix that soon with styling prompts.

Take a look at the code to verify that the fetch URL includes your API key and looks correct. If Bolt made any other mistakes (for example, a typo in the endpoint or not using the key properly), this is a good time to catch them. A quick way is to open the browser's developer console and see if there are any errors. You might get a "401 Unauthorized" notification if the key was wrong, for example, or a 404 if the URL is wrong. If everything's correct, there should be no errors and the movies should display.

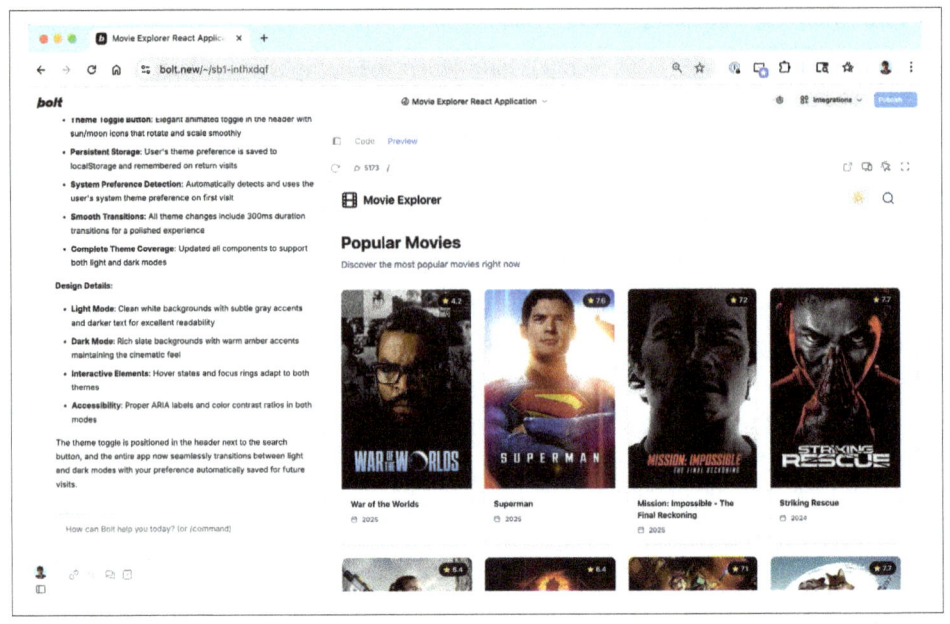

Figure 5-2. The Movie Explorer app in preview, showing the main home page with movie posters, release years, and rating stars

If you ever want to check what Bolt's generated in detail, you can open the file it edited and look at the code. It might look like this:

```
import { useState, useEffect } from 'react';

const TMDB_API_KEY = "YOURKEY...";

function Home Page() {

  const [movies, setMovies] = useState([]);

  useEffect(() => {

    fetch(`https://api.themoviedb.org/3/movie/popular?api_key=${TMDB_API_KEY}`)

      .then(res => res.json())

      .then(data => setMovies(data.results))

      .catch(console.error);

  }, []);

  return (

    <div className="movies-grid">
```

```
    {movies.map(movie => (

      <div key={movie.id} className="movie-card">

        <img src={`https://image.tmdb.org/t/p/w200${movie.poster_path}`}
        alt={movie.title} />

        <h3>{movie.title}</h3>

      </div>

    ))}

  </div>

  );

}

export default Home Page;
```

Even if you don't fully understand this code yet, it's basically what I just described: it fetches data on load, then renders each movie's poster and title.

Adding a Search Feature

Next, let's allow users to search for movies by title. Our home page will get a search bar (text input) where the user can type, and we'll fetch matching movies from TMDB's search API.

TMDB's search endpoint is */search/movie?query=YOUR_QUERY*. We will need to call that when the user submits a search. Let's prompt this:

Add a search bar at the top of the home page. When a user enters a movie name and submits, search TMDB for that title and update the list to show the search results instead of popular movies.

We're asking Bolt to:

- Create a search input (and possibly a button, or make it so pressing Enter works).
- Capture the search term from the user.
- Use the TMDB search API to fetch movies matching the query.
- Replace the displayed list with the results.

Bolt will add an input field (and maybe a form or button), possibly in JSX. It might look something like this:

```
<input

  type="text"

  placeholder="Search movies..."

  value={searchTerm}

  onChange={e => setSearchTerm(e.target.value)}

/>

<button onClick={handleSearch}>Search</button>
```

This introduces a state for searchTerm (e.g., via useState('')) and a handler, handle Search. The handleSearch function will use fetch to call TMDB's search endpoint:

```
fetch(`https://api.themoviedb.org/3/search/
movie?api_key=${TMDB_API_KEY}&query=${searchTerm}`)
```

Bolt will process the JSON and update the movies state with the results, similar to before. (It might decide to implement the search on form submit instead of using a button. Both are fine. The key is that it triggers the fetch when the user wants to search.)

Our code should also handle edge cases: if searchTerm is empty, maybe it should fetch the list of popular movies again, or do nothing. But that might be extra; if Bolt doesn't address it, we can refine.

After implementing that, Bolt will likely modify the component's return JSX to include the input and button at the top, above the movie grid, as can be seen in Figure 5-3.

Now we can test the search functionality. Once Bolt updates the code, try it out in the preview. Type a movie name, like *Inception*, and hit the search button. The app should call the API and update the display. You might briefly still see old movies until the new results come in. For simplicity, Bolt's code might not show a loading indicator, but if the request is fast, that's fine.

If nothing happens when you search, do the following:

- Check that the search input or button is present.
- Try pressing Enter, in case Bolt added a form that requires hitting Enter.

- An error in the console may indicate that Bolt forgot to call `event.prevent Default()` on form submit. By default, submitting an HTML form reloads the page; calling this function prevents that behavior, allowing our React code to handle the submission instead. We can fix that by prompting Bolt to handle the form submission properly.

- If the `searchTerm` isn't being picked up, make sure you click the button after you type it.

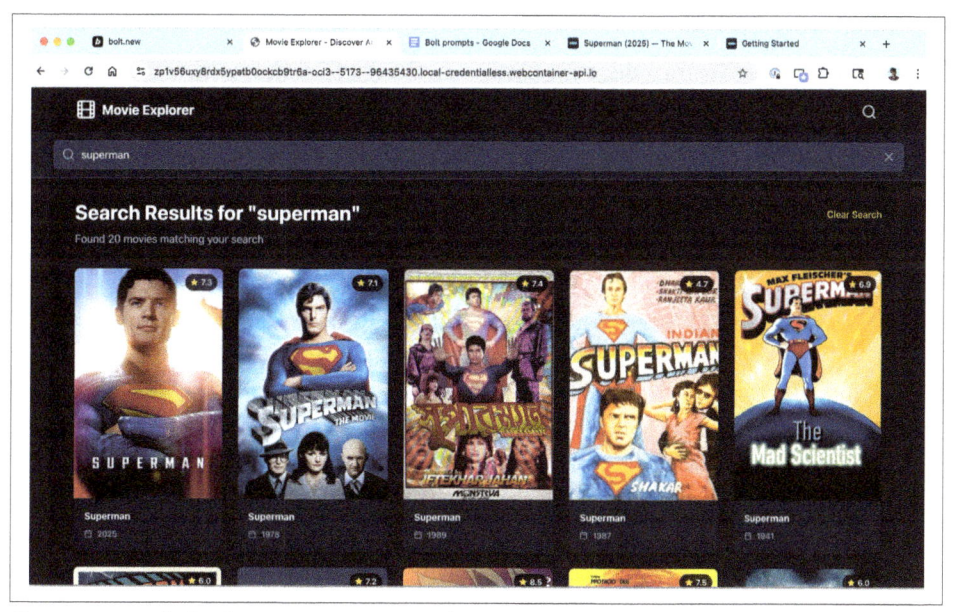

Figure 5-3. Bolt displays a responsive grid of movie cards matching a search query for "Superman"

Typically, Bolt does a decent job here. We may want to refine the UX: for instance, after search, maybe it should have a "Back to popular" option or automatically show popular movies when `searchTerm` is cleared. But let's keep it simple and instruct Bolt to show the popular movies if `searchTerm` is empty:

> If the search input is empty, show the popular movies list again by default.

This makes the app more user-friendly, since users aren't stuck with the results of their last search results. Bolt could implement this by adding a `useEffect` dependency on `searchTerm` or, if `searchTerm` is an empty string, a condition in `handle Search` to fetch the popular movies list.

Now our home page supports both initial popular listing and searching.

Implementing the Movie Details Page

We now have movies displaying, but clicking on them currently does nothing. We want a dedicated page or view to show more details about a movie when selected. This new component or page will fetch detailed information for that movie ID (TMDB has the endpoint */movie/{movie_id}* to provide these details) and display it. For example, if a user clicks on *The Dark Knight*, our app should show a page with a full overview, release date, quality rating (on a scale of 1 to 10, or perhaps 1/2 star to 5 stars), and a larger poster.

To do this, we need to introduce navigation (routing) in our app. Each movie item should be clickable and should navigate to a route associated with that movie, using the movie's unique ID in the URL (such as */movies/12345*).

We didn't explicitly tell Bolt what framework to use or which library to use for routing. If it used Next.js for the project, it might have set up file-based routing. If it's a single-page app instead, Bolt might need to install React Router to handle client-side routes. Let's take a look. After our initial code has been generated for the movies app, check if *package.json* has `next` or `react-router-dom`. If `next` is present, Bolt has used Next.js, so it might prefer using Next.js's pages. If `react-router-dom` is present, Bolt is doing a single-page application (SPA) with React Router.

Either way, let's instruct Bolt accordingly to make our movies more interactive:

> Make each movie item clickable. When a movie is clicked, navigate to a details page for that movie and display its details (using TMDB's movie details API). Include the movie's poster, title, overview description, release date, and rating on the details page. Provide a back link to go back to the home page.

We're asking for a lot. Bolt should:

- Add a clickable wrapper or link around each movie in the list.
- Set up a route for the detail view.
- On that detail route, fetch the movie's details by ID and display them.

Let's see what Bolt does.

If Bolt Chooses React Router

For this example, it chose to use React Router, so the rest of this section will follow that path. If your app is using Next.js, skip to the next section.

Bolt installs `react-router-dom` since it was not already installed. (You can check if it was needed by looking at Bolt's logs.) Then it creates a routing setup in `App.js`, something like this:

```
<BrowserRouter>

  <Routes>

    <Route path="/" element={<Home Page />} />

    <Route path="/movie/:id" element={<MovieDetailsPage />} />

  </Routes>

</BrowserRouter>
```

For the clickable wrapper, in the `Home Page`, it has wrapped the movie items in `Link` components from `react-router-dom` so that clicking on a movie item will change the URL and show the movie details:

```
<Link to=
    {`/movie/${movie.id}`} key={movie.id} className="movie-card"> ...
</Link>
```

Bolt has created and implemented a new component, `MovieDetailsPage`, for the details view. Its implementation fetches the details via `useEffect` and uses `useParams` (from React Router) to get the `id` from the URL:

```
fetch(https://api.themoviedb.org/3/movie/{id}?api_key=TMDB_API_KEY).
```

In response to the final sentence of our prompt, Bolt also added a simple backlink at the top:

```
<Link to="/"> Back to home</Link>
```

Consider including logic for loading states and error handling. Bolt may not automatically add a dedicated loading indicator—instead, it might simply delay rendering content until data arrives. To avoid UI flicker or confusion, proactively implement minimal loading feedback and graceful error fallback.

If you would like to display fallback loading or skeleton UI while the movie details components and their children are loading in, React Suspense (*https://oreil.ly/kNOQX*) is what you would use to achieve this in a React app. If Bolt has not implemented such UX and you're noticing latency, you can ask it to help here via a prompt:

> Can you add some React Suspense fallbacks to the loading of my MovieDetailsPage component and its children, such as gray boxes?

If Bolt Chooses Next.js

If Bolt chose to use Next.js for your implementation, it will start by creating a file in the *pages* directory, likely named with a unique movie ID: [id].js or similar. Next.js automatically maps the route /movie/[id] to that file.

Bolt might then use getServerSideProps, client fetch, or a combination of the two—or possibly client fetch in a React component, for simplicity.

The backlink on the home page would be done with Next.js's syntax:

```
<Link href={/movie/${id}} />
```

The rest—fetching data and displaying the movie details—is similar to what I described in the React section.

Testing the Details Page

After this prompt, our app gains the ability to show details. To test that out, click on one of the movie posters on the home page. The URL in the preview might change to include that movie's ID: *.../movie/12345*. The page should show the movie's details, including the title, a poster, and the overview text (a few paragraphs from TMDB). You might see additional info like "Release Date: 2020-07-16" or "Rating: 8.3/10."

Find the back link and click it too. It should return you to the home page, with the popular movies list or your search results. If not, something is off. Let's troubleshoot:

- If clicking does nothing, make sure Bolt actually implemented the link. Try manually refreshing the preview's URL to the movie route to see if the page works. If Bolt forgot to wrap with <Link>, we could prompt it again specifically to "wrap movie items in proper links."

- If the details page is blank or giving an error, open the console for hints. Maybe the fetch failed. Did Bolt use the correct id in the URL?

- Sometimes you need to check to make sure the app is actually using React Router—that is, that it's rendered in the index. This isn't an issue for Next.js.

At this point, you have a pretty complete Part 1 of the app, with a home page that shows a list of popular movies and a search bar, and you can navigate to a movie's details page for more info (Figure 5-4).

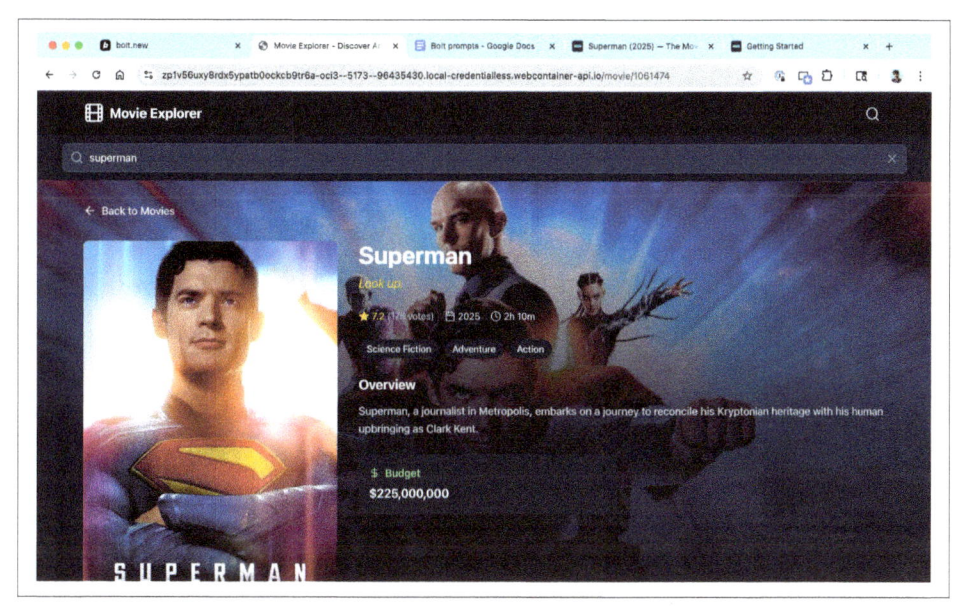

Figure 5-4. A detailed movie page generated by Bolt, showing an individual film's metadata and budget

Polishing the UI

Bolt now takes care of many responsive and design features by default, including generating nice navigation and headers. However, once you have your basic Movie Explorer app functionality working, there are many polish touches that can elevate the user experience from functional to delightful. These enhancements focus on the finer details that make an app feel professional and engaging. This list offers some example prompts for enhancing the UI:

Visual polish and microinteractions

Small animations and visual feedback can make your app feel more responsive and alive. Consider asking Bolt to add subtle transitions and hover effects:

Add smooth hover effects to movie cards—when users hover over a movie poster, gently scale it up by 5% and add a subtle shadow. Also add a fade-in animation when the movie grid loads.

Create loading states with skeleton screens while movie data loads. Show gray placeholder rectangles that shimmer where the movie posters will appear.

Add a subtle pulse animation to the search button when users are typing in the search field, and show a small loading spinner inside the button when a search is in progress.

Enhanced search experience

Beyond basic search functionality, you can create a more sophisticated search experience:

Implement search suggestions that appear in a drop-down as users type. Show recent searches and popular movie titles as they start typing.

Add search filters with animated toggles—let users filter by genre, release year, and rating with smooth sliding toggles and animated checkboxes.

Create a "no results" state with a friendly illustration and suggested alternative searches when no movies match the user's query.

Improved navigation and discoverability

Help users navigate and discover content more intuitively:

Add breadcrumb navigation that shows "Home → Search Results → Movie Title" with clickable arrows between each level.

Create a "Recently Viewed" section on the home page that shows the last 5 movies the user looked at, with small thumbnail previews.

Add a floating "Back to Top" button that appears when users scroll down the movie list, with a smooth scroll animation when clicked.

Content enhancement

Make the movie information more engaging and useful:

Display movie ratings with interactive star components—show filled and empty stars based on the rating, and add a subtle glow effect on hover.

Add movie genre tags as colorful pills beneath each movie title, with different colors for different genres (action movies get red tags, comedies get yellow, etc.).

Create an expandable movie synopsis on the details page—show just the first two lines by default with a "Read More" link that smoothly expands to show the full description.

Accessibility and user comfort

Enhance the app for different user preferences and needs:

Add a dark/light mode toggle in the header with a smooth transition animation between themes. Store the user's preference and remember it for their next visit.

Implement keyboard navigation—users should be able to tab through movie cards and press Enter to view details, with clear focus indicators.

Add text size options in a settings menu—small, medium, and large text sizes that users can choose from for better readability.

Advanced interactive features

Create more engaging ways for users to interact with content:

Add a "Favorites" heart icon on each movie card that fills with red when clicked and saves to a favorites list accessible from the header.

Create a movie comparison feature—let users select multiple movies and view their ratings, genres, and release dates side by side in a comparison table.

Implement a movie recommendation carousel on the details page—show "Movies similar to this one" with horizontally scrollable cards.

Performance and polish

Optimize the user experience with thoughtful loading and feedback:

Add progressive image loading with blur-to-sharp effect—show a blurred version of movie posters first, then crisp versions as they load.

Create smart pagination for the movie list—load more movies automatically as users scroll near the bottom, with a subtle loading indicator.

Add error handling with friendly messages—if movie data fails to load, show a retry button with a helpful message like "Something went wrong. Let's try that again."

These polishing touches transform a basic functional app into something that feels professional and enjoyable to use. The key is to think about every moment of user interaction and consider how small improvements can create a more delightful experience. Bolt can handle these kinds of detailed UI improvements effectively, allowing you to focus on the user experience rather than implementation details, as you can see in Figure 5-5.

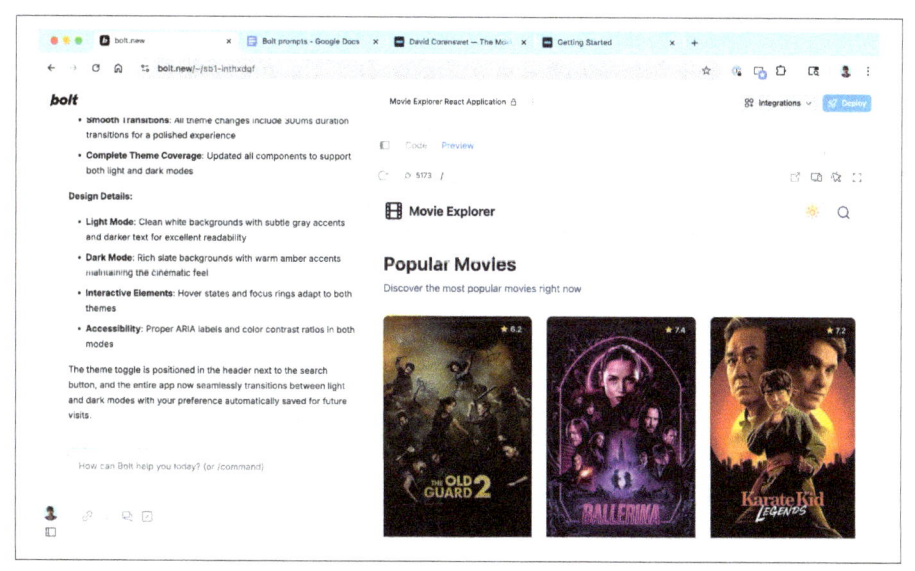

Figure 5-5. Light-mode view of the Movie Explorer app with popular movies and a clean UI, demonstrating how thoughtful UI polish elevates the user experience

You can gradually refine styling by describing the changes, or "change the background to dark mode" and Bolt will adjust the CSS. For example:

Make the titles font larger.

Change the background to dark mode.

It's an iterative design process. Just like an artist might tweak a painting brushstroke by brushstroke, you tweak your app's appearance prompt by prompt.

Testing the Application

Now it's time to play with your creation and ensure it works as expected. When you first load the app (or when you clear the search), do you see a list of movies? It should show current popular titles. Scroll through and make sure that their images and titles appear, and that the layout is OK, the posters aren't cut off, and so on.

Test the search functionality by searching for a few movies. The search term "Spider-Man" should bring up a variety of Spider-Man movies.

Search for something obscure or a misspelling, too, to see how the app handles TMDB returning an empty list. This app, as it currently stands, would just show nothing in the grid if TMDB returned no movie matches. We could further improve the UX by showing a "No results found" message if the movie list is empty after a search. We can prompt Bolt to add:

If the search returns no movies, display the message "No movies found."

Bolt will add a conditional rendering to show that message whenever `movies.length === 0`.

Clear the search field and confirm that the list of popular movies comes back (if you implemented that logic).

To test the movie details, click on a few different movies from either the popular list or your search results. Confirm that their details pages load and that they show the correct movie's info, and compare them.

Use the back link or header link to return and try another movie. Try navigating directly too. If you can manually edit the URL in Bolt's preview, pick an ID from one of the movies (so you know it exists) and try navigating to it this way. The app should fetch and show that movie's page.

The overall experience should feel like a small version of using IMDB (*https://imdb.com*) or another movie directory: you can find movies and read about them.

Is everything working? Great! If you do encounter any issues, this is the time to address them by adjusting with prompts or making minor code edits. For example, if the mobile layout isn't ideal, you could instruct Bolt to make some specific responsive changes. Or if some images are broken and you found a movie that had no poster, you could instruct Bolt on how it should handle missing images:

Show a placeholder image if `movie.poster_path` is null.

Common Issues and Troubleshooting

Here's a quick rundown of common issues you might run into while building this app with Bolt, and how to handle them:

Incorrect API key or "Unauthorized (401)" errors
If no movies show up and you see an error in the console about "Unauthorized" or "Invalid API key," double-check that you inserted your API key into the code correctly. If it's missing or you made a typo, prompt Bolt again to add the key string properly, or open the code editor and manually correct it. Remember, the key must exactly match the one from TMDB, with no extra spaces.

Cross-origin resource sharing (CORS) errors when fetching API
Occasionally, APIs can have cross-origin resource sharing (CORS) restrictions. TMDB's API is generally open for client-side requests, so you shouldn't face CORS issues with the correct endpoints. If you do, it might be a network or URL issue; ask Bolt's Discussion Mode for help. For TMDB, though, this is unlikely to be a problem.

Routing to details pages is not working
If clicking a movie doesn't take you to its details page, make sure the link is set up. If you're using React Router, the app might need to be wrapped in `<Browser Router>` only once (having multiple routers can break navigation). You should find this in *App.jsx* or *index.js*. If Bolt forgot about this issue, you can explicitly prompt it:

Wrap the app with a router so that links work.

Refreshing the details page gives a 404 error (on a deployed environment)
In development, Bolt's dev server handles routes, but if we were to deploy this (which we will in Chapter 7), directly accessing a client-side route (like */movie/123*) might require configuration. Using Next.js avoids this because routes are known, but if you're using React Router on a static host, you might need a redirect rule. I'll show you how to handle that in Chapter 7, which is about deployment. For now, in Bolt's environment, it should work because the dev server catches all routes.

Styling issues

> If the grid or details layout isn't looking right, adjust your prompts: if posters are too large, specify a smaller width. If text is too close to edges, ask for padding. Don't be afraid to be picky. Think of Bolt as your junior web designer who's very accommodating about your pixel-pushing directives.

Exceeding Bolt's token limit

> In rare cases, if you give a very large instruction or the codebase becomes big, Bolt might hit its AI token limit. Bolt provides free tokens daily (*https://bolt.new/pricing*) as part of its free plan. If it stops responding, you might have hit the limit. You can wait for the next day or consider upgrading to a paid plan, which has much more relaxed usage limits.

Discussion Mode

A great feature of Bolt is Discussion Mode (*https://oreil.ly/g_G1J*), where you can ask Bolt questions about the code it wrote. For example:

> Is there a bug in the search function? I'm not seeing results.

What makes Discussion Mode special is that it is context-aware and internet-equipped: the AI can look up the latest guidance or documentation and answer with references. Bolt uses Google's Gemini 2.0 model for this mode, which is optimized for answering questions and can cite sources.

After it answers, you'll often see quick action buttons like "Implement this plan" or "Show an example." If you click "Implement this plan," Bolt switches back to the regular build mode and applies the code changes the discussion answer suggested, effectively turning the advice into action. This feature is incredibly powerful for beginners: you can use Discussion Mode to learn *why* something is done or get confirmation on an approach, and then seamlessly carry those changes into your app. It's a safe sandbox to deepen your understanding without "using up" your prompt tokens on trial and error. And because it can pull in external info, it stays current.

It can even analyze its own code and help debug it, much like a colleague would. Don't hesitate to use it if you're stuck.

You can resolve most issues by clarifying your instructions to Bolt or doing a tiny manual tweak.

Tips and Best Practices

While building Movie Explorer, we've touched on several best practices that will be useful going forward:

Prompt specifically and iteratively

Bolt works best when you give it specific goals then refine the results. We started with a broad prompt to scaffold this project then added features one by one. This stepwise approach helps Bolt "understand" the project context progressively and reduces errors. If you ask for too many things at once, Bolt might miss some details or get overwhelmed, just like a human would.

Leverage real APIs and data for realism

Using the TMDB API made our app functional and interesting. When you're building apps through Bolt, connecting to a known service like a weather or news API is a great way to get real content. It also teaches you how to work with external data.

Review and understand the generated code

Even if you're not coding manually, take a moment to read the code Bolt produces. This will help you pick up on how things are structured, like the `fetch` call and the state update. Over time, you'll start recognizing patterns (like `useEffect` for on-load actions). This knowledge will empower you to guide Bolt better, and even fix or tweak code on your own if needed.

Test frequently

After each significant change, we tested the app's functions, searching for movies and clicking on links. This is important because if something goes wrong, you catch it early, and your next prompt can address it. Think of testing as part of the conversational flow with Bolt: you observe then instruct accordingly.

Use Bolt's context window to your advantage

Bolt remembers the previous code it wrote, up to a certain point. You can reference things you've mentioned in previous prompts, like "the movies state" or "that grid style," and Bolt will usually understand which part of the current project you mean. This is very convenient—you don't have to specify every detail again.

Stay mindful of limitations

Bolt is powerful but not infallible. Sometimes it produces code that doesn't run the first time or forgets to follow best performance practices, like refetching too often. Part of the reason humans oversee the process is to catch those mistakes and correct them. As you've seen, it's worth adding conditions to avoid unnecessary requests (like not searching repeatedly if a query comes up empty). Bolt might not think of everything, so your role is to steer it.

Keep your API keys safe

I've mentioned this, but as a best practice, don't commit API keys to a public repository or expose them in a deployed app (see Chapter 7); usually, you'd set keys in an environment config on the server. For learning, it's fine, but be cautious in real projects.

Use the documentation and communities

If you're unsure how to do something, you can ask Bolt. But don't hesitate to look through official documentation too. For instance, if you want to add information about actors, you might need to consult the TMDB docs for an endpoint. Bolt itself was likely trained on documentation. Online communities are a great resource too: other developers have likely asked the same questions you're wondering about.

Summary

Congratulations! You've built the first part of the Movie Explorer app using Bolt, without writing code by hand. Let's recap what you achieved in this chapter:

- You used Bolt to scaffold a React-based web app by describing your desired application in a prompt.
- You integrated your app with an external API (TMDB) by providing an API key, and then let Bolt handle the fetch calls and data rendering.
- You implemented core features through natural language instructions, which Bolt translated into working functionality: displaying popular movies in a grid, searching for movies by title, and viewing detailed information on a separate page.
- You added basic styling and layout to make the app presentable.
- You tested the app and debugged issues through an iterative process, using both Bolt's help and your own observations, which is a realistic development workflow.
- Finally, you learned some best practices for prompting and guiding an AI development tool, such as breaking tasks down, being specific, and reviewing the generated code.

That's a lot to accomplish. Well done!

Your Movie Explorer app is already useful: you can search for information on thousands of movies. In Chapter 6, we'll enhance this app further by introducing user accounts (authentication) and a favorites feature, so users can save a list of movies they like. We'll integrate Bolt with a backend service (Supabase) for storing data and see how to manage user-specific content. This will transform Movie Explorer from a read-only reference tool into a personalized application.

Before moving on, feel free to experiment with the app you've created. Try adding more fields to the details page, like genres or running times. You can change the styling too: maybe a dark theme? This app is a sandbox where you can practice prompting. The more you play with Bolt, the more comfortable you'll get with its capabilities.

Keep your TMDB API key and Bolt instance handy, and let's continue our journey in building with Bolt!

CHAPTER 6

Building a Movie Explorer App, Part 2: Favorites and Authentication

In this chapter, we extend the Movie Explorer app from Chapter 5 with two major features: favorites and authentication. This means users will be able to create an account and, while logged in, mark movies as favorites. The app will save these favorite movies and allow the user to view their personal favorites list any time, from any device (as long as they log in to their account). Ideally, you'll have your Chapter 5 project open in Bolt. We will add to it from there. If for some reason you didn't do Chapter 5, Bolt can generate a starting point if you prompt it, but for continuity, I'll assume you have the Movie Explorer app working, including search and details.

These features are important because authentication adds a personal experience. Users can have their own data (like favorites), and the app can distinguish one user from another, like how you log in to Netflix to get your own watchlist. This is foundational for any multiuser application. And the favorites feature introduces a simple database usage into the app. When a user favorites a movie, that information must be stored somewhere persistent (so it's not lost when the app reloads). We'll use Supabase, a popular backend as a service that provides a database, authentication, and storage. Bolt integrates with Supabase out of the box (*https://oreil.ly/BNRMW*). Supabase essentially gives you a cloud database (using PostgreSQL under the hood) and user auth system with very little setup.

By the end of this chapter, Movie Explorer will evolve from a browse-only app into a more interactive, personalized web app. Users will be able to:

- Create a user account (or use a dummy test account)
- Log in and log out of the app
- While logged in, mark some movies as favorites

- See a list of their favorite movies (with details like poster and title) on a separate page or section
- Unfavorite (remove) a movie from their favorites list, if desired

Also by the end of this chapter, you'll understand how Bolt handles integration with a database and authentication service with minimal coding.

This chapter will also provide a gentle intro to backend concepts for nontechnical readers. We'll discuss how data is stored in tables (like spreadsheets in the cloud), how each user's data is kept separate and secure using user IDs and authentication, and how data flows from the app to the backend (when favoriting a movie) and back into the app (when retrieving favorites).

It sounds complex, but I'll show you how Bolt makes it much simpler by doing a lot of the heavy lifting, such as connecting to Supabase and writing the code to interact with it. You'll still be guiding Bolt with clear instructions and learning a bit about what's happening under the hood.

Supabase Setup

Before implementing favorites and auth, you'll need to create a Supabase account, connect Bolt to Supabase, set up a Supabase project, and get a Supabase API key.

Create a Supabase Account

Supabase offers a free tier. Sign up (*https://supabase.com*) with GitHub or an email. Bolt's integration will actually let you sign in directly, but having console access is useful for setup.

Connect Supabase with Bolt

Bolt can connect to Supabase. On the Bolt home page or project page, find Settings → Applications → Supabase and click Connect. Bolt will prompt you to log in with Supabase. Use the Supabase credentials you just set up. This authorizes Bolt to manage your Supabase projects (don't worry—it will only do what you instruct it to).

After connecting, in your Bolt project interface, you should see a Connect to Supabase option (a button or link at the top right).

Set Up a Supabase Project with a Favorites Table

To get started with Supabase (*https://oreil.ly/U7yLn*), you need to create an organization and then create a project within that organization. Supabase allows you to manage multiple projects under a single organization. This setup helps in organizing your work and managing different aspects of your applications.

When you create a project, Supabase generates a project URL, something like *https://xyzcompany.supabase.co*. It also generates an anonymous public API key, or *anon key*: a long string, typically starting with ey. You'll need to provide these to Bolt so the app can communicate with Supabase.

It's OK to include the anon key in your frontend code, because it's safe (*https://oreil.ly/Uu8zv*) when used with *row-level security (RLS) policies* (*https://oreil.ly/0yf6y*). RLS ensures that users can only access the data they're allowed to see. Think of it as a gatekeeper that checks every query! There's also a more powerful service role key (*https://oreil.ly/aHWfP*), but that one bypasses RLS and should only ever be used on a secure backend—not in Bolt's frontend code.

You'll need to decide how you want to structure your favorites data. For this example project, we'll take a simple approach: creating a table (or collection) named Favor ites that stores which user has favorited which movies. Each Favorites entry will have:

- An id (primary key)
- A user_id (to identify the user who saved it)
- Some movie info (at least a movie_id from TMDB, maybe the title or poster for convenience)

By default, Supabase provides an auth.users table to store user accounts, and it gives each user a unique id. That user_id is what we'll use to link the Favorites table to each user.

Here's how to set up the Favorites table through the Supabase web UI:

1. Create the table. In your Supabase project dashboard, go to Table Editor and create a new table called favorites.

2. Add a user_id column (UUID). Set the type to UUID. If the UI lets you, check the box to link it as a foreign key to auth.users.id. If not, just store the UUID manually.

3. Add a movie_id column. TMDB IDs are integers, so use integer for the movie_id column.

4. Optional: Add movie_title and poster_path (text). This duplicates data but makes the app faster and simpler by not requiring extra TMDB API requests when showing favorites.

5. Add a timestamp column named created_at. Set its default value to now() to track when each favorite was added.

6. Set the primary key. Supabase will default to adding a unique `id` column (integer or UUID). You can keep this default—it's fine for unique row identification.

7. Enable RLS. This must be turned on to safely use the anon key along with user-specific data access. Enabling RLS means no one can access the table until specific policies are set.

8. Create user-specific policies. Supabase provides templates for these, like "Users can select/insert their own rows." Use a policy such as `CREATE POLICY ...` `USING (user_id = auth.uid());` for both `SELECT` and `INSERT`. This ensures that each logged-in user can only see or add rows where `user_id` matches their UID.

User Segregation: UID Versus UUID

A *universally unique identifier* (UUID) is a 128-bit string (like `3f1e8a2f-...`) that's globally unique across systems. UUIDs are ideal for `user_id` storage.

User ID (UID), in Supabase, refers to the authenticated user's ID from `auth.uid()`, which is also a UUID. So in practice, Supabase compares your `user_id` column (UUID) to your `auth.uid()` (UID) to enforce row ownership.

Using RLS with policies like `user_id = auth.uid()` ensures that each user only accesses their own rows, preventing anyone else from seeing or altering them. This is called *user segregation*. You can think of it as a digital fence that separates user data automatically—no manual checks are needed in your frontend.

By following these steps and enabling RLS with proper policies, you'll have a secure `favorites` table. Each user will:

- Only be able to see or add their own favorites
- Use the frontend-safe anon key
- Avoid leaking or accidentally sharing data with other users

Supabase's documentation and UI will assist you with these steps. The RLS part is crucial for security, but if it's too much, you could disable it during development. This would mean that any user could see everyone's favorites, so it's not good for production, but it's fine for testing purposes. However, I want you to do it properly, to illustrate best practices.

Once set, the Supabase anon key (which Bolt will use in the frontend) can only access the `Favorites` table through the allowed policies.

Integrate Authentication with Supabase

Alright, let's start by integrating Supabase for authentication. This feature addition is more involved than earlier ones, so budget some time and be patient. We'll effectively be doing full stack work (frontend and backend integration), but Bolt will simplify much of it.

Have your Movie Explorer project from Chapter 5 open and running. If you closed it, you might have a Bolt share URL or project saved; if not, you can quickly regenerate it by following the steps in Chapter 5 or summarizing them to Bolt, which might be able to rebuild it quickly. Ideally, you'll continue with the same project and keep the code.

The first step is to add user accounts to our app so people can sign up with email and password and then log in. Supabase's authentication looks a lot like other well-known systems—it handles user data in the database and gives you easy APIs for signing up, logging in, and logging out. You don't need any prior experience with Firebase or any other platform to get started—it's straightforward and easy to learn.

In your app, you can set up the login/sign-up flow however you like—either on a separate /login page or in a pop-up modal. To keep things simple in this tutorial, we'll use a dedicated /login page.

Connect the Bolt Project to Supabase

Before writing prompts for code, you need to ensure Bolt knows your Supabase project details. If you used Settings → Applications → Supabase → Connect, Bolt is now authorized.

Next, within your Bolt project, click "Connect to Supabase" (Bolt's UI likely shows this option when Supabase is connected globally). Bolt should prompt you to either use an existing project or create a new one. Choose the project you created in Supabase (it might show by name).

Once connected, Bolt might automatically inject your Supabase credentials into the environment or project and/or install the @supabase/supabase-js library, the official JavaScript client for Supabase. Check if Bolt has added something like a *supabase* folder or a config file with the URL and anon key behind the scenes.

Bolt can now use Supabase.

Prompting Bolt to Add an Authentication UI

Now it's time to start prompting. Instruct Bolt to create a sign-up and login system:

> Add user authentication to the app using Supabase. Create a page or modal for users to sign up or log in with email and password. Include fields for email and password and buttons to Sign Up and Log In. Once logged in, the app should show the user's email (or a welcome message) and a logout option, instead of the login form.

That's a long prompt, but we want Bolt to handle multiple pieces, including:

- The UI for signing up and logging in (we can have them on one page for simplicity—maybe a toggle, or just two forms)
- Calls to `supabase.auth.signUp({...})` and `supabase.auth.signIn({...})`, Supabase's auth functions
- Maintaining the auth state (knowing who a user is and if they're logged in or not)
- Changing the UI after login (hiding the auth form and showing "Hello, *user@example.com*" and a logout button)

Bolt should create a new component or page called something like `AuthPage.jsx` or add logic to the app. If the Supabase JavaScript client is not already installed, it will do that, then initialize it with our project URL and anon key. This could be in a config file or right in the code, like this:

```
import { createClient } from '@supabase/supabase-js';

const supabaseUrl = "https://YOURID.supabase.co";

const supabaseKey = "YOUR_ANON_KEY";

const supabase = createClient(supabaseUrl, supabaseKey);
```

If Bolt has the environment ready from when you connected it to Supabase, it might use that instead of hardcoding, likely with an environment variable or a provided object.

To create the UI, it will probably create a form with `email` and `password` inputs and two buttons (or one button that switches mode), as shown in Figure 6-1. When clicked, these buttons will call Supabase. For sign-up, this will be something like `supabase.auth.signUp({ email, password })`. For sign-in, it will be `supabase.auth.signInWithPassword({ email, password })`. The API may vary if you're using newer versions of the Supabase client. If signing up requires email verification, Supabase by default will send a confirmation email.

Once the user logs in, Bolt stores the logged-in state. It may use `useState` to hold user, or use `supabase.auth.onAuthStateChange` to track if a user is logged in. It will also modify the main app or header to reflect the user's auth status. If a user is present, it will show a greeting and a Logout button. If not, it will show a Login link or button to open the auth form (Figure 6-1). Finally, it will implement logic to call `supabase.auth.signOut()` when the user clicks on Logout.

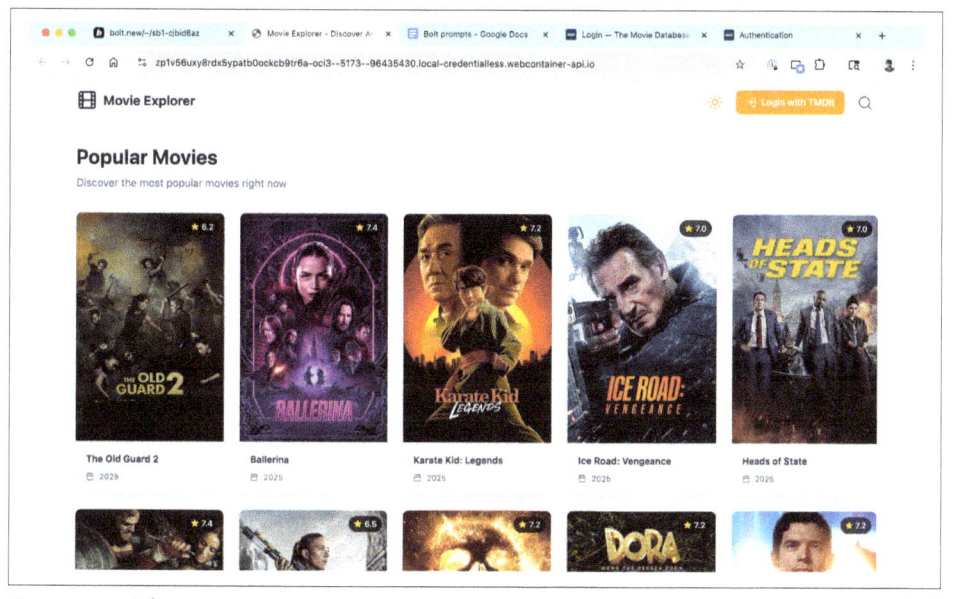

Figure 6-1. The Movie Explorer app prompting the user to log in using TMDB credentials

That's quite a lot for Bolt to do at once. It will probably do most of what we've asked, but we may need to refine some of the results. For instance:

- If Bolt provides a separate */login* page, we might want to change this to something simpler, like a single page with a form that handles both registration and login. After login, we can have Bolt navigate back home or just hide the form.

- If Bolt doesn't do so, we may need to add a "Login" option to the header for when no user is logged in.

- If Bolt provides two separate forms for sign-up and login, we could prompt it to just do one form (with separate buttons but the same credentials fields) that signs up new users and logs in existing ones.

After making any refinements to Bolt's attempt, let's test it out. The app should now show a login form (Figure 6-2). Try signing up a new user (use a test email like *test@example.com* and a simple password) and watch the Bolt console (maybe add a `console.log` on error) to see if it succeeds. Supabase typically returns either the user or an error.

If email confirmation is turned off, the user is logged in right away. If confirmation is on, the user field might be null and you'll get something like "verification email sent." For our learning purposes, you can disable email confirmations in Supabase Auth settings by turning off the "confirm email" requirement, so that sign-up logs in the user directly.

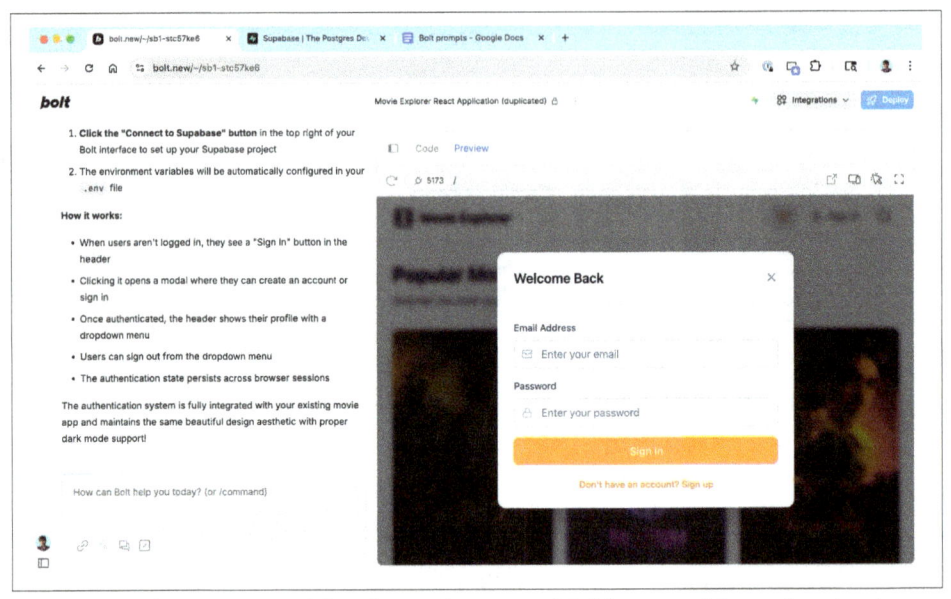

Figure 6-2. The Sign In modal with email/password fields, part of the authentication flow

Next, try logging out and logging back in with the same credentials. Once you've logged in, the UI should indicate it with something like "Welcome, *test@example.com*!" (See Figure 6-3.) Make sure the login form is gone.

If something fails, check if the Supabase client was initialized with the correct URL and API key. Since we used Bolt's connect feature, it might not show the keys in code (they may be stored in an environment that Bolt manages). If it's not working, try explicitly giving Bolt the key in a prompt:

> Use this Supabase URL and key to initialize the client: [url] [key]

Also, check that the site URL configured in Supabase Auth includes `localhost` (or whatever domain Bolt's preview uses), because Supabase by default might restrict redirects. Bolt likely uses a form of `localhost` for the web container. In Supabase Settings → Auth → URL Configuration, add *http://localhost:3000* (substituting the appropriate domain if needed) as an allowed URL. Otherwise, you could get an error on the OAuth or magic link (though for emails and passwords it's usually fine).

You should also check that, on refresh, if you're logged in, Supabase retains the session. (It uses local storage for the token.) Bolt's dev server might reset if the container restarts, but if it maintains a continuous connection, the Supabase client `auth.getUser()` or similar could retrieve the session. Bolt can implement that.

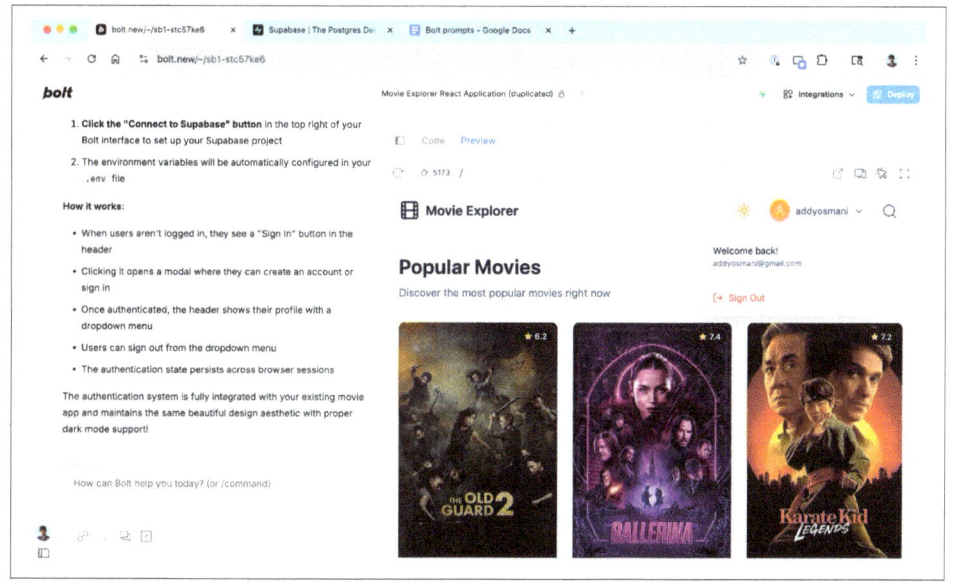

Figure 6-3. After login, the app header includes the user's profile, email, and a sign-out menu

This is a critical stage. Once user authorization is functioning, working with favorites becomes easier because we have a `user_id` to tie them to. Now that the basics are resolved, we're ready to tackle favorites.

Implementing Favorites Functionality

With auth in place, we can now allow logged-in users to save their favorite movies to a list of favorites. Here's what we'll ask Bolt to do:

- Add a "Favorite" button (this is often a heart icon or star) on movie listings and details pages.
- Guard actions so only logged-in users can favorite movies—so if the user clicks the Favorite button but is not logged in, the app should prompt them to log in.
- When a logged-in user clicks Favorite, the app should record that favorite in Supabase.

- Provide a way for the user to see their favorites list. This could be a separate page called My Favorites with a grid that lists all their favorited movies with posters, titles, and so on, similar to the home page grid.

- Allow users to "unfavorite" movies (remove them from the favorites list) by clicking the heart again or clicking a remove button on the favorites page.

Let's proceed step by step.

Add a Favorite Button on Movies

Where can users favorite movies? We want to put an "Add to Favorites" button on each movie's details page. We could also put one on each movie card on the home page by overlaying a small heart icon on each poster (Figure 6-4).

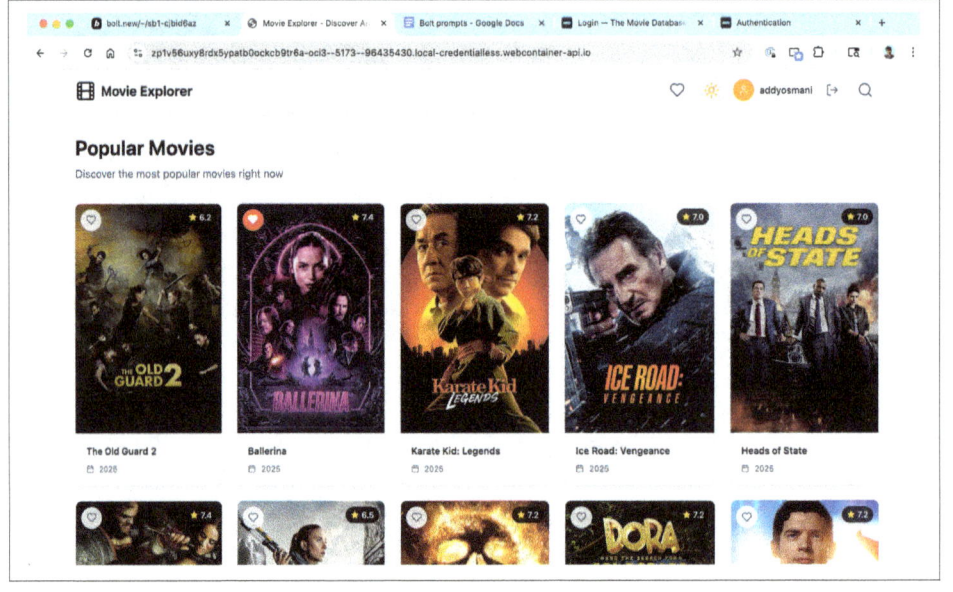

Figure 6-4. The home page view after logging in, showing favorite icons activated for some movies

For now, let's add it to the details pages:

> On the movie details page, add an "Add to Favorites" button. If the user is not logged in, clicking it should prompt them to log in (e.g., redirect to login page or show a message). If the user is logged in, clicking it should save the movie to the user's favorites in Supabase (in the favorites table with `user_id` and movie info). Change the button state or text to indicate the movie is favorited after clicking.

This prompt instructs Bolt to include a button on `MovieDetailsPage` that says "Add to Favorites."

To check that the user is logged in, Bolt will add an onClick handler that checks authentication. If there's no logged-in user, it may navigate to the login page or show an alert, like "Please log in to favorite movies."

Your component (in this case, MovieDetailsPage) needs access to the current logged-in user. There are three ways to do this. You can:

- Pass the user object in as a prop
- Use global state
- Use React Context to share user info across your app

Bolt's generated code should check whether that user value is truthy before deciding how to handle the click. *Truthy* refers to a value that is considered equivalent to true in a Boolean context, even though it may not explicitly be the Boolean value true itself.

If the user is logged in, Bolt will add logic telling the app to call Supabase to insert a record into the favorites table:

```
supabase.from('favorites').insert({

  user_id: user.id,

  movie_id: currentMovie.id,

  movie_title: currentMovie.title,

  poster_path: currentMovie.poster_path

});
```

The currentMovie data should still be available from when we fetched details; it's likely stored in state on the details page. Once the favorite is added to the database, the app should disable the button or turn it into Favorited.

Bolt might also handle errors: for instance, if the user has already favorited this movie, Supabase might either insert a duplicate or, if we set a unique constraint, an error. We could prevent duplicates by making user_id and movie_id unique in DB, but that's not required for this tutorial; we can handle it in the UI by disabling the favorite button after one favorite.

Now it's time to test the new feature! First, test the favorite button while logged out: you should get a message telling you to log in, or the app might navigate to the login page. To prompt Bolt to redirect to login, do a secondary prompt if needed:

> If a user tries to favorite while not logged in, redirect them to the */login* page, and after login, bring them back to the movie detail they were on.

Next, log in, navigate to a movie details page, and click "Add to Favorites." Check Bolt's logs or check the `favorites` table data in the Supabase web UI to see if the entry was added. You should see a row with your user's UUID and the movie ID.

Has the button changed to Favorited or become disabled? Try refreshing the details page. The app may not remember the movie's state unless we have it query the database (which we haven't implemented yet). If that's the case, the button might revert to "Add to Favorites" because the component doesn't know the movie was favorited already. We'll implement a favorites page where this will be more persistently visible.

Add a My Favorites Page

Now we'll create a page where the user can view all their favorite movies. This page essentially reads the list from the database and shows those movies in a grid similar to the home page:

> Create a My Favorites page that lists all movies the logged-in user has favorited. Each favorite should show the movie's poster and title (just like the movie cards). Allow the user to click a favorite to go to that movie's detail page. Also, include a remove button (or unfavorite icon) on each, so the user can remove it from favorites. Only logged-in users can access this page; if not logged in, prompt to log in.

Bolt should make a new component called `FavoritesPage`. On load, this page will fetch an array of favorite entries from Supabase for the current user:

```
const { data: favorites } = await supabase.from('favorites')
.select('*').eq('user_id', user.id);
```

We stored `movie_title` and `poster_path`, so we can display those directly. If we want up-to-date info and don't mind making more API calls, we could alternatively tell Bolt to fetch full movie details via TMDB for each favorite. The app will render the list, similar to how the `HomePage` does with the list of popular movies:

```
favorites.map(fav => (

  <div key={fav.id} className="movie-card">

    <img src={`https://image.tmdb.org/t/p/w200${fav.poster_path}`}
    alt={fav.movie_title} />

    <h3>{fav.movie_title}</h3>

    <button onClick={() => removeFavorite(fav.id)}>Remove</button>

  </div>

))
```

The new `removeFavorite` function will call Supabase and then update state to remove the movie from the list (Figure 6-5):

```
supabase.from('favorites').delete().eq('id', favId)
```

Bolt should also wrap each item in a link to the film's details page (`/movie/{movie_id}`) so the user can click its card in the grid to see details if they want.

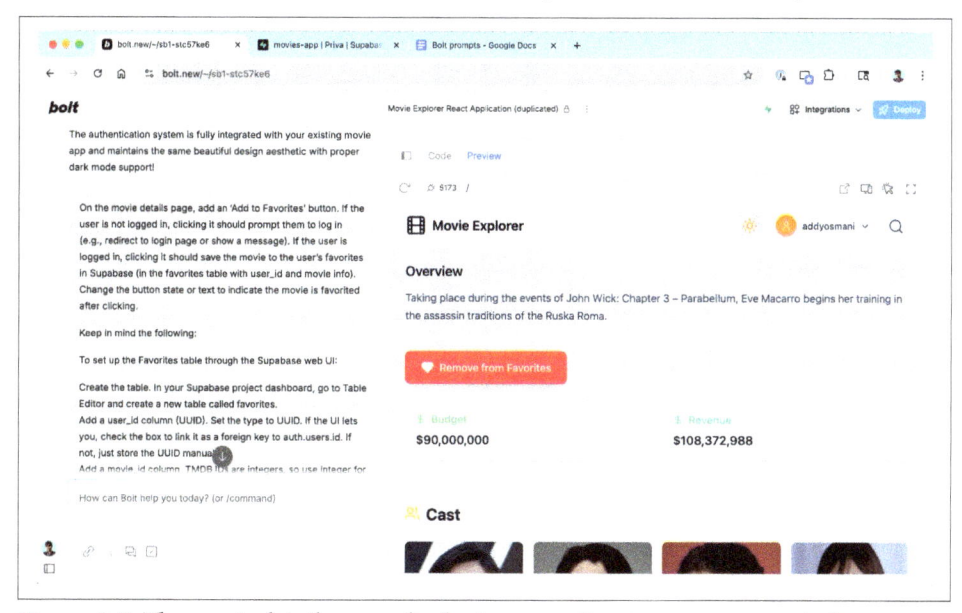

Figure 6-5. The movie detail screen displaying an option to remove a movie from favorites

As with the button, if the user clicks on the My Favorites list but isn't logged in, the app should either redirect them to the login page or show a message like "Please log in to view favorites."

Bolt will also add a link to this Favorites page in the UI, probably in the header or navigation bar. If you're using React Router, define a route `/favorites to FavoritesPage`. If you're using Next.js, create `pages/favorites.js`.

After implementing all that, it's time once again to test. Log in and favorite a couple of movies via the details page, like you did before. Then navigate to My Favorites via the link Bolt added or manually if the link is missing. You should see a list of the movies you favorited, along with their posters (Figure 6-6). If the favorites list doesn't show anything even after you add movies, maybe the fetch didn't run or the data wasn't stored correctly. Check if the `user.id` in the `favorites` table matches the Supabase user's ID exactly (they should, if we inserted everything correctly).

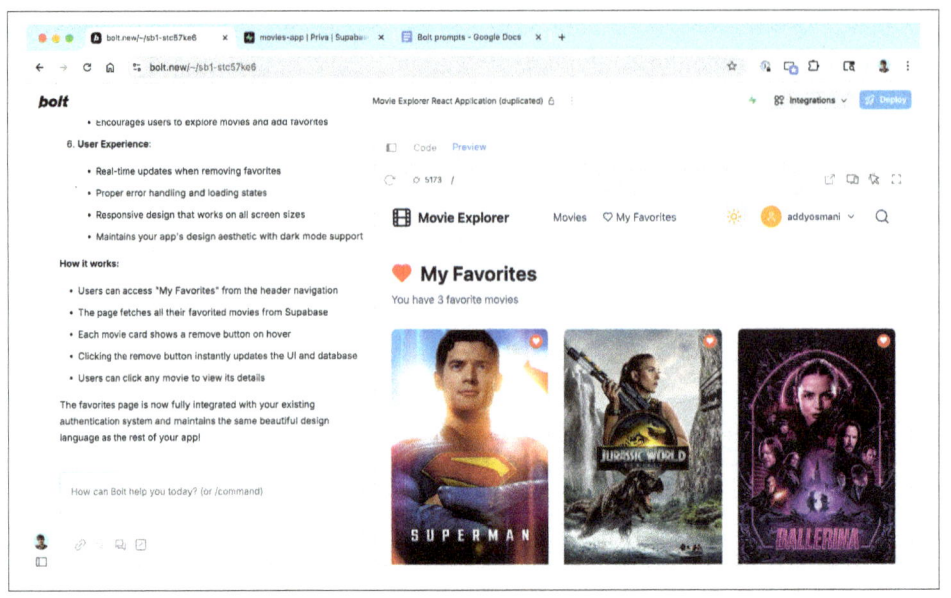

Figure 6-6. The My Favorites page listing movies saved by the user, fetched from Supabase

Click Remove on a favorited item and it should disappear from the list. Check the Supabase table to ensure that the entry was deleted. Try clicking a favorited item's image or title as well; it should go to the details page of that movie.

Now log out, and then try to go to My Favorites by entering the URL. The app should stop you or show an empty state with a login prompt.

After logging out, check that the Favorites page and any other user-specific data have been cleared from state. Bolt might not automatically clear the `favorites-list` state on logout. We've told it to simply not render the favorites page if the user is logged out, so it will rely on a fresh fetch when they log in again.

If RLS is enabled with the correct policy, our Supabase calls will only return the current user's data, which is good. If not, any user's client could technically get *all* users' favorites by modifying the query (which is bad). So make sure RLS is on, especially in production.

For testing, if RLS causes permission errors (401) on selecting or inserting favorites, the policy isn't letting it perform those actions. Perhaps Bolt forgot to set the `user_id` on insert? If the insert has the `user_id` null or wrong, the policy will deny permission to select or insert favorites. Our code explicitly sets this policy, but if a new user's sign-up is not confirmed, `auth.uid()` might not match. We'd debug by checking `error` from Supabase calls.

Common Issues and Troubleshooting

Here are some potential issues you might face and how to fix them.

Authorization issues

Authentication can be tricky. These are common problems with sign-up, login, and account handling:

Email not accepted
> If you see an error like "Email already registered" (from Supabase) on sign-up, use a different email or log in using that email instead. If the error is "Invalid login credentials," double-check you typed your email correctly. We didn't implement a "reset password" function in this tutorial, so if you forget the test password, just sign up again with a new email.

Nothing happens when you click sign-up or login
> Open the browser console (DevTools) to see if an error was thrown; maybe the Supabase library didn't load. Check also that Bolt included the Supabase script; since we connected via their integration, it should. If not, you may need to run `npm install @supabase/supabase-js` in Bolt's terminal manually, or prompt Bolt to do so.

The UI doesn't update when you log in
> If logging in seems to work but the UI doesn't update, maybe Bolt didn't use a state or context to refresh the component. Fix this by manually calling `supa base.auth.getSession()` or using the `onAuthStateChange` callback to update the user state whenever the session changes.

Favorites insertion issues

Sometimes the UI is unresponsive due to missing libraries or silent errors. Here's how to debug those cases.

If clicking favorite yields an error or doesn't reflect the change, check the network and console. Did Supabase return a permissions error? You may be using RLS without a proper policy. The fix: ensure that the policy allows the insert.

If our code didn't send the `user_id` at all, the insert might fail if the `user_id` field requires a non-null value. If Bolt forgot to include `user_id`, adjust the prompt or code to include it.

Favorites retrieval issues

Is your favorites list empty when it shouldn't be? The problem may be in how the user ID is queried or how the data is fetched:

The My Favorites page is empty
> If the favorites page shows as empty even though the table has data, filtering the query by user_id might not match if user_id is stored as anything other than a UUID string. In the JavaScript client, check that the favorites.user_id values and the user.id match exactly.
>
> It could also be that Bolt forgot to call .select() properly or didn't wait for the async. If you suspect the fetch code might be wrong, prompt Bolt to double-check it or add a console log of the data.

Removing a favorite doesn't work
> If removing a favorite doesn't actually remove it from the UI, it could be that the state update after deletion wasn't implemented: that is, Bolt might have removed from Supabase but not filtered the local state. Make sure the code updates the favorites state list after anything is deleted. For example:
>
> ```
> setFavorites(favorites.filter(f => f.id !== deletedId)));
> ```

You could also have it refresh the list from the database after a deletion (this is simple if less efficient).

Navigation and state issues

If the app doesn't redirect the user to the home page (or wherever they came from) after they log in, ensure that the app knows they've logged in. Bolt may or may not handle the redirect. If not, prompt it:

> Navigate to home after successful login.

It might have a lot of moving parts, but you now have a functioning favorites system.

Tips and Best Practices

Working with authentication and databases brings new considerations. Here are some tips and best practices I've observed:

Secure your data with proper rules
> We used Supabase's RLS to ensure each user can only access their own favorites. This is crucial in multiuser applications. If you use another backend, implement similar permission checks. Bolt makes integration easy, but always double-check that your backend isn't inadvertently exposing user data.

Don't expose sensitive info on the frontend

Our app uses an anon key, which is meant to be public (it's scoped by RLS), so we haven't exposed any secret keys. If you use any admin-level keys, never put them in frontend code or version control.

Streamline the login/sign-up process

For instance, after sign-up, log the user in directly or at least tell them to check their email if verification is needed. If Bolt didn't add error messages on the form in case sign-in fails, you can easily add a state for an error message and display it. A friendly UX makes a big difference.

Keep track of user state

When using an auth system, maintain a single source of truth for whether a user is logged in. The Supabase client can do this via `onAuthStateChange`. We could register a listener once and update a global state. That way, any part of the app can react to login/logout. Bolt might have done something like this:

```
supabase.auth.onAuthStateChange((event, session) => {
  setUser(session?.user || null);
});
```

This ensures that the UI updates if, say, a session expires or the user logs out from another tab.

Plan for logged-out versus logged-in views

We modified our header to show "Login" or "My Favorites/Logout" depending on state. Always consider what parts of an app should be gated. In our case, Favorites is gated, but we've allowed browsing and searching without login (which is fine).

Consider performance

We did an extra fetch to get favorites on page load. If that data was frequently needed (like showing a star next to each movie in a listing if it's favorited), we might want to fetch favorites once globally and reuse it to avoid calling the database too much. But given the likely low volume, this straightforward approach is acceptable.

Clean up resources

In a long-running app, like a multipage React app, it's best practice to clean up any event listeners when those parts of the UI unmount. Otherwise, you can run into memory leaks or unexpected behavior. If you don't unsubscribe from event listeners, after a component unmounts (that is, the user navigates away), the Supabase auth listener may still be active. If it tries to update state by calling `setUser(null)` on a component that no longer exists, React will warn you that it "can only update a mounted or mounting component."

When using `supabase.auth.onAuthStateChange(...)` in a `useEffect`, the function returns an object containing a `subscription.unsubscribe()` method. You should call that cleanup in your effect's return:

```
useEffect(() => {  const { data: authListener }
    = supabase.auth.onAuthStateChange((event, session) => {
    // handle session change
});
    // Cleanup when the component unmounts
    return () => {
       authListener.unsubscribe();
      };
}, []);
```

This prevents the listener from firing after you leave the page. It also eliminates memory leaks and avoids console warnings. For Bolt-generated code in a single-page setup, this may not be strictly necessary, but in any React app with multiple pages or unmounting components, it's a good habit to include it.

Summary

With Part 2 completed, our Movie Explorer app is robust. Users can now create accounts, search for movies, view details, and maintain a list of favorites that persists across sessions. This is a big step up in complexity, yet we achieved it with relatively few prompts and without writing low-level code ourselves. It's a testament to how much heavy lifting a tool like Bolt can handle, connecting a frontend to a backend seamlessly.

You now have a fuller application that mimics real-world app capabilities (account management and persistent user-specific data). This is a major milestone: you essentially built a mini version of something like a "watchlist" feature on a movie site.

From a learning perspective, you also got introduced to how the frontend and backend communicate: you've seen how the frontend (React via Bolt) made calls to Supabase (backend as a service) to store and retrieve data. You dealt with asynchronous operations (fetching from the network, waiting for a response) and, like most apps, used an external service for auth instead of building one from scratch.

You've built a fully functional, full stack application with Bolt, all within your browser and through plain English commands. Pretty cool, right? Take pride in that achievement as we move on to making this app live for the world to see in Chapter 7.

Deploying Your App with Netlify Integration

Up to now, we've been running our Movie Explorer app in Bolt's development environment (essentially on your local machine, through the browser). Now it's time to deploy the app, which means making it accessible on the internet with its own URL. We will use Netlify to host our Movie Explorer. Netlify is a popular hosting platform for modern web projects, particularly Jamstack apps. It automates building, deploying, and serving websites and web applications.

Deployment can be a tricky step in traditional development (involving servers, configurations, CI/CD pipelines, and the like), but Bolt's integration with Netlify (*https://oreil.ly/dZ-Xh*) simplifies it to just a few clicks. Bolt's integration means that we can trigger the deployment from within Bolt's interface. Bolt will handle packaging the app (running the build step) and sending it to Netlify. Netlify will then host it on a public URL (likely something like *your-app-name.netlify.app*, though Netlify does support custom domains as well).

This chapter will guide you through:

- Connecting your Bolt project to Netlify
- Deploying the app (with a look at what actually happens under the hood during deployment)
- Verifying the live site and testing all features on production
- Managing any configuration needed for production (like environment variables for API keys)
- Making the deployment process repeatable, so you can update the site as you improve the app

By the end, you'll have your Movie Explorer app live online, which is a huge accomplishment. You'll be able to share it with friends or add it to your portfolio.

Deployment Steps

Optionally, you might want to push your code to a GitHub repository or another Git host for version control. Bolt has an export or download option. This isn't strictly needed, since we'll deploy directly from Bolt in this chapter.

Let's get started!

Connect and Configure Netlify in Bolt

Before we begin, make sure your codebase is deployment-ready. This includes making sure you've set all necessary keys (your TMDB API key and Supabase URL and key) in your code or environment. The app should run without errors in Bolt's preview.

If you don't have a Netlify account yet, sign up (*https://netlify.com*) (you can use an email or log in via GitHub). The free tier is sufficient for our needs.

Next, we need to get Bolt connected to Netlify, similar to how we connected Supabase. On Bolt, go to Settings → Applications, find Netlify, and click Connect. It will ask for your Netlify login and permission. Authorize it.

If you've introduced any build configurations (like in Next.js) or if you're using any environment variables, you might have to configure them on Netlify. Our app uses a TMDB API key and a Supabase anon key, both of which we embedded in the code (not ideal security-wise, as discussed in Chapter 5, but OK for now).

You've already connected Netlify in Bolt's settings. Now, within the Bolt project, click the Deploy button at the top-right corner of the page. Bolt will automatically generate a site name for you (something like *effulgent-prosciutto-123456.netlify.app*). You can keep this default name or customize it later through your Netlify dashboard under Domain Management.

Monitor the Deployment Process

After you click Deploy, Bolt's interface should show the build output (Figure 7-1). Watch for it to declare build success or alert you to any errors. If there's an error, fix it before continuing.

You won't see detailed deployment logs within Bolt itself. Instead, to monitor the deployment process and view logs, you'll need to check your Netlify dashboard. Select your newly created site, then click on Deploys to see the deployment history. Click on the latest entry to view the full deploy log.

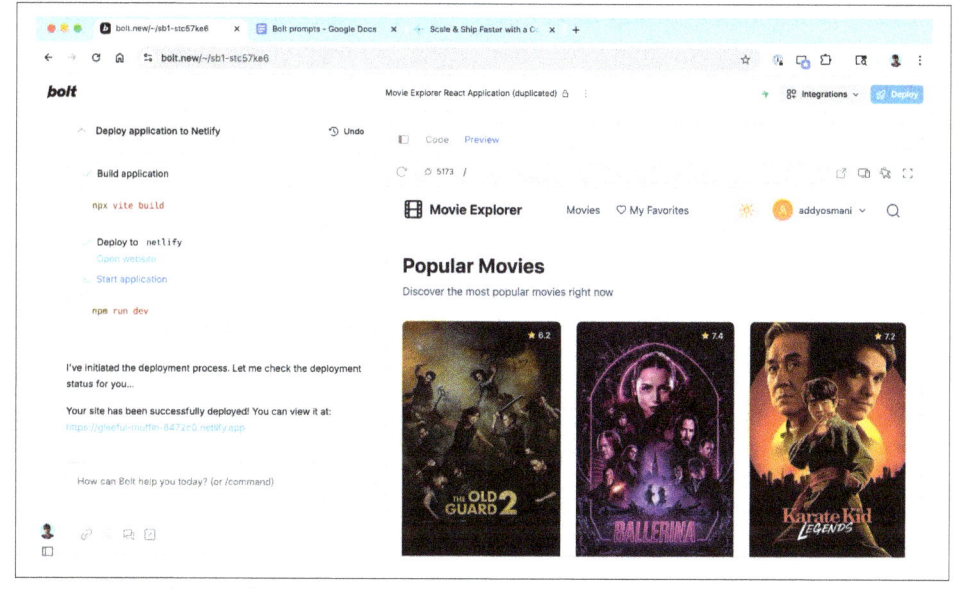

Figure 7-1. Bolt completes a Netlify deployment and provides a link to the live app

Under the hood, Bolt is packaging your built files and sending them directly to Netlify through its API. Netlify then processes the deployment and provides detailed logs showing the installation of any production dependencies and the build process (for React apps, likely `npm run build`; for Next.js, building the app and prepping functions). Netlify hosts the final output and provides a URL.

You don't need to manually set up a site on Netlify's dashboard; Bolt does it for you. Bolt's chat interface will give you the URL once deployment is complete.

Test the Live Site

Once deployed, visit the URL Bolt gives you, which will be something autogenerated, like *movie-explorer-1234.netlify.app*.

Now you can test all of your app's functionalities as a real user. Start by making sure the home page loads and shows the list of popular movies. Try a search to make sure that functionality works.

Click a movie card to navigate to that movie's details page. Then try visiting directly, by manually entering a details page URL in a new incognito window or new tab to see if it loads. If it doesn't and you get a Netlify 404 error, see "Common Issues and Troubleshooting" on page 91.

Next, test the login and sign-up functions on the live site. This is a big one, because now we're using the production URL. Here's what you need to know about authentication on your live site:

- For basic email and password logins, this should work fine right away. Supabase won't block your new Netlify address for simple email/password authentication.
- If you decide later to add features like "Sign in with Google" or magic email links that let users log in with one click, you'll need to tell Supabase which website addresses are allowed to receive users after they sign in. You do this by adding your Netlify URL to the "Redirect URLs" section in your Supabase project settings under Authentication.

After logging in, test the favorites functionality. Open the Supabase dashboard, then add a favorite—you should see it appear on the dashboard.

Go to the My Favorites page and verify that it loads. Try logging out and see that protected routes (like the My Favorites page) are blocked, as expected.

Open the Netlify link on your phone to test its responsiveness on mobile, if you can. The design might not be fully responsive, since we didn't specifically style for that. If something is off, note it as a potential improvement.

Everything should behave the same way it did when you were testing in Bolt's preview environment. In other words, the live site should work exactly like the development version you were building—same features, same data, same user flows, with no surprises or missing functionality.

Customize the Netlify Deployment (Optional)

You can change the site name to something readable and unique (let's say "My Movie Explorer"), if you want to. If you plan on sharing the app with others or on a resume, a custom name or domain looks nice. To do so, log in to Netlify.com, go to Sites, and find your deployed site (it should be there, since Bolt used your account). In Site settings, you'll see an option to change the site name. This will also change the URL (*my-movie-explorer.netlify.app*). You can also add a custom domain if you own one (Netlify provides instructions for that (*https://oreil.ly/kSRl-*)).

You can also do continuous deployment through Netlify. If you link a Git repo and push code, Netlify can autobuild. In our case, if we continue using Bolt to make changes, we could redeploy via Bolt each time. Alternatively, now that it's on Netlify, we could download the code from Bolt, push it to GitHub, and then connect Netlify to that repo for CI/CD. That's outside Bolt's direct flow but might be good to know.

Make Post-Deployment Updates

Remember, deployment isn't a one-and-done; it's an iterative process. You might decide to implement improvements to Movie Explorer, now that you can quickly see them live.

Whenever you update the app in Bolt (or directly in the code), you'll need to redeploy to see those changes live. Bolt should let you redeploy to the same site easily. Our first deploy set up the site, and subsequent deployments will update it. Keep track of any versioning you do or changes you make, since this will help you debug any issues later on.

For example, if after deployment you notice a bug (say, the search bar doesn't align nicely on mobile), you can go back to Bolt and fix the CSS via a prompt. Test the fix in Bolt's dev preview, and then hit Deploy again. Netlify will update the site within seconds.

This tight loop is extremely powerful: you have an idea, you implement it with Bolt, and within minutes, it's live to the world.

Common Issues and Troubleshooting

As much as Bolt streamlines deployment, there are always a few things that can go wrong:

You get a 404 error
  If you're using React Router, direct navigation to a route like */movie/123* on Netlify might result in a 404, because Netlify will try to find a file called *movie/123*. To fix this, Netlify needs a redirect rule to route all requests to *index.html* (which our app then handles through client-side routing). This is usually done via a *_redirects or netlify.toml* file. Bolt might have added that if it detected a single-page app. If it didn't, add a *_redirects* file:

```
/*    /index.html   200
```
  Then you can test and redeploy.

  If you added a custom domain, you had to configure DNS according to Netlify's instructions. If you didn't do that correctly, your site might not resolve, which would result in a 404. Follow Netlify's domain instructions or just stick with the *netlify.app* domain for simplicity.

The My Favorites page doesn't work
  If you get a "not allowed" error or your data doesn't show when you try to load My Favorites, check that the `auth.uid()` works. If you had email confirmation off during development but you've turned it on in production, new sign-ups from the live site might require email confirmation. Adjust accordingly in your

Supabase settings; you may want to turn off confirmation for now to make testing easier.

The build fails
If the deploy log in Bolt shows a failure, read the error: was a module not found? Does the code have a syntax or case-sensitivity error that somehow didn't surface in development? Fix it accordingly in Bolt (it will generally offer a "fix" button) and try again.

Something that worked in development doesn't work in production
Check your API keys: Are they present and correct in production? (We embedded ours, so they should be.) You can open the DevTools on the live site and inspect network calls: see if the URL for Supabase requests is correct and if there are any errors.

Once you've ironed out any kinks, you have a stable deployment pipeline: Develop in Bolt → Deploy to Netlify → Use and share the live site. Well done!

Tips and Best Practices

If your app gets popular, monitor its API usage:

- TMDB's API has a rate limit; at this writing, it's about 40 requests every 10 seconds. Our app making a request on each search or detail view should be fine, unless someone spam-clicks. If your usage grows, TMDB might require an API key upgrade or request caching.

- Supabase's free tier has limits on database rows and bandwidth, which should be fine for a demo with a few users. If you've invited many users, watch those or upgrade to a higher tier.

- Netlify's free tier offers generous bandwidth and build minutes for small apps. If your app's usage spikes, they might notify you and ask you to upgrade to a higher tier.

It's not common to lose a Bolt project, but since it's in the cloud environment, you might want to export and download the project code. That way, you have a local copy. Also, it's good practice to commit your code to a Git repository if you can.

If a new deploy introduces a bug, Netlify allows you to roll back to a previous deploy with one click. So if something goes awry and you don't have time to fix it immediately, you can temporarily restore the last good version. Remember, always test after deploying to catch issues.

Once your app is live, you can add things like Google Analytics or Sentry error tracking by inserting their scripts or using their packages. Bolt can even help integrate those. This is beyond the scope of this book but worth noting as a next step for professional apps.

I mentioned earlier that Netlify handles both static and dynamic content well. Here's what that means in practice:

Static content
Consists of files that are prebuilt during deployment—your HTML, CSS, and JavaScript files. Netlify serves these directly to users' browsers, making them load very quickly. When someone visits your Movie Explorer, they immediately get the basic page structure, styling, and interactive code.

Dynamic content
Information that changes based on the user or gets fetched in real time, like the movie data from TMDB or a user's personal favorites from Supabase. This content isn't built ahead of time. Instead, your JavaScript code requests it from APIs after the page loads in the user's browser.

This approach, called the *Jamstack (https://jamstack.org)*, gives you the best of both worlds: fast initial page loads from static files, plus personalized, up-to-date content through API calls. You get the speed and security benefits of static hosting while still supporting user accounts, real-time data, and interactive features.

Historically, deploying an app with a backend and frontend has involved setting up a server, a database, and so forth. With Bolt and Netlify (and Supabase for the backend), everything is serverless and managed, allowing even nonexperts to put an app online quickly.

Summary

In this chapter, we took our Movie Explorer from a development setup to a production deployment. You learned about Netlify's hosting features, environment variables, and site settings. We also established a workflow for future updates: develop locally with Bolt, then deploy to Netlify when ready. This means you can roll out improvements continuously.

At this point, you have a fully functional, deployed web application. Congratulations! This is a huge milestone. You can share the Netlify link with anyone, and they can use your app. Think about that: in just a short time, you've gone from idea to live product, using natural language and a bit of guidance from a smart tool.

Feel free to continue enhancing the Movie Explorer. Here are some ideas:

- Add pagination or infinite scroll so users can browse more than the first page of popular movies.
- Include more info on the details pages, like cast or trailers—the TMDB API has those.
- Use a star rating component to let users rate movies themselves and save those ratings.
- Integrate a social feature like commenting (this would require more backend work, maybe using Supabase or a third party like Disqus).
- Polish the UI with animations or a more responsive layout, maybe creating a CSS framework via Bolt prompts.
- Implement OAuth login through Supabase to allow users to log in via Google or GitHub to avoid managing passwords. Supabase and Bolt can handle that, with a little more configuration.

Each of these could be an exercise with Bolt in itself.

You now have the foundation and the confidence to build and deploy full stack apps using Bolt and a few helpful services, without manually coding everything. In the next chapters, we'll explore different kinds of apps you can build using Bolt, to expose you to more integrations and use cases.

In Chapter 8, we'll create a Supabase-powered workout tracker (diving deeper into database usage and maybe even adding some serverless functions for custom logic). In Chapter 9, we'll use Figma integration to build a grocery list app, showcasing how Bolt can take designs and turn them into code automatically. These will further solidify your skills and show the breadth of what's possible with Bolt. Until then, take pride in the fully deployed app you've created, and get ready for more Bolt magic!

CHAPTER 8

Building a Supabase-Powered Workout Tracker

Now that you've seen what Bolt can do with a movie app, let's try another practical project: a workout tracker. This application will allow users to log their workouts (exercises, reps, sets, and the like), track progress, and manage their fitness data. We'll leverage Supabase extensively here—not just for authentication, like in the movie app, but for our primary workout-data storage. We'll use a relational database design.

The goal of this chapter is to demonstrate how Bolt can help build a more data-intensive application from scratch, with a heavy focus on using a database (Supabase) for storing and retrieving structured information. Unlike the movie app, where the data came mostly from an external API, here the central feature will be our own app's data in the form of workout logs.

Getting Started

By the end of this chapter, you'll have a functional workout tracker where users can:

- Create and manage workout sessions with multiple exercises
- Log exercises with sets, reps, and weights
- View past workouts ordered by date
- Delete workout sessions
- See a summary of their workout activity
- (Optional) Visualize progress with charts

- (Optional) Experience real-time updates across devices
- (Optional) Use Edge Functions for server-side calculations

Setup

If you worked through the Movie Explorer chapters, you've already done most of the setup: you have accounts for Bolt, Supabase, and Netlify, and you've connected them. If not, see Chapters 5 through 7 for detailed instructions.

For this project, create a new Supabase project called "WorkoutTracker" (the free tier allows two active projects). Start a new Bolt session for this app, and in Bolt's settings, connect to your WorkoutTracker Supabase project.

Planning the Data Schema

Before we start coding, let's design how we'll store workouts in Supabase. A well-planned database design will make querying and managing data much easier as the app grows.

We'll use a relational approach with two tables: `workout_sessions` (Table 8-1) and `workout_exercises` (Table 8-2). This creates a one-to-many relationship where each workout session can contain multiple exercises. This design offers several advantages:

- Clean data organization
- Easy aggregation of exercise data
- Flexibility to add features later
- Proper normalization avoiding data duplication

Table 8-1. Fields in the workout_sessions table

Field	Data type	Description
id	UUID (Primary Key)	Unique identifier using `uuid_generate_v4()`—a PostgreSQL function that generates random 128-bit identifiers
user_id	UUID (Foreign Key)	References `auth.users.id` to link each session to a user
session_date	Date	The date of the workout
title	Text	Optional session name like "Leg Day" or "Upper Body"
created_at	Timestamp with time zone	Automatically set to current time, useful for sorting

Table 8-2. Fields in the workout_exercises table

Field	Data Type	Description
id	UUID (Primary Key)	Unique identifier for each exercise entry
session_id	UUID (Foreign Key)	Links to workout_sessions.id—this creates the parent-child relationship
exercise_name	Text	Free text field for exercise names (e.g., "Bench Press," "Squats")
sets	Integer	Number of sets performed
reps	Integer	Repetitions per set
weight	Numeric	Weight used (you'll standardize on kg or lbs)
notes	Text (nullable)	Optional field for comments like "felt easy" or "new PR"

Some of the key design decisions are as follows:

- The session_id field in workout_exercises references the id in workout_sessions, creating referential integrity.
- We only store user_id in workout_sessions, not in workout_exercises, avoiding redundancy.
- We're using free text for the exercise names right now. Later, you could create a separate exercises table for standardized names, if you like.

Setting Up Tables in Supabase

1. Navigate to the Table Editor in your Supabase dashboard.
2. Create the workout_sessions table with the fields from Table 8-1.
3. Create the workout_exercises table with the fields from Table 8-2.
4. Set up the foreign key constraint from workout_exercises.session_id to workout_sessions.id with CASCADE on delete.

Implementing Row-Level Security (RLS)

RLS is crucial for ensuring users can only access their own data. This section shows how to set it up.

RLS for the workout_sessions table

Enable RLS in the table's settings. Then create a policy for all operations:

```
CREATE POLICY "Users can manage their own sessions"

ON workout_sessions

FOR ALL
```

```
USING (user_id = auth.uid())

WITH CHECK (user_id = auth.uid());
```

The USING clause ensures that users can only read rows where they are the owner; the WITH CHECK clause lets users only insert or update rows with their own user_id.

RLS for the workout_exercises table

Create a policy that checks ownership through the parent session:

```
CREATE POLICY "Users can manage exercises in their sessions"

ON workout_exercises

FOR ALL

USING (

  session_id IN (

    SELECT id FROM workout_sessions

    WHERE user_id = auth.uid()

  )

);
```

Supabase provides quick-start templates for these common patterns. Look for "Enable insert access for users based on user_id" in the policy templates.

Building the Workout Tracker

Now, armed with our data schema and security rules, let's build the app with Bolt.

Scaffold the project

Start with a comprehensive prompt to Bolt:

> Create a new React web application called Workout Tracker. Use Supabase for authentication and data storage. The app should use two related tables: workout_sessions (id, user_id, session_date, title) and workout_exercises (id, session_id, exercise_name, sets, reps, weight, notes). Users should be able to create workout sessions, add exercises to them, view their past workouts, and delete sessions. Include user authentication with email/password.

This prompt tells Bolt about our two-table structure up front, ensuring it generates appropriate code for the relational design.

Set up authentication

Guide Bolt to implement auth first:

> Implement user sign-up and login using Supabase Auth. The app should require login. Provide a form for email and password sign-up/login, and show a logout button when logged in. After logging in, redirect to the workout dashboard.

Test the authentication flow in Bolt's preview (Figure 8-1). If email confirmation is blocking your testing, temporarily disable it in Supabase's Auth settings.

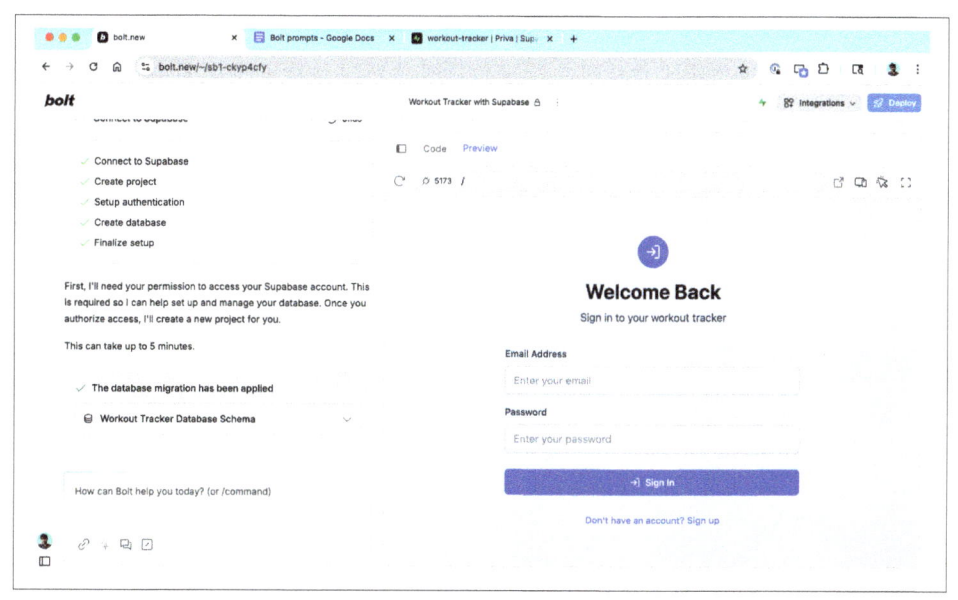

Figure 8-1. Bolt shows Supabase setup completed, with login screen for the workout tracker

Creating workout sessions

The workout creation process involves two steps: creating a session, then adding exercises to it. Let's prompt for the session form:

> Add a form to create a new workout session. Include fields for date (default to today) and optional title. When submitted, insert into the workout_sessions table with the current user's ID. Store the new session's ID in state to use when adding exercises.

Adding exercises to a session

Once a session is created, users need to add exercises:

> After creating a session, show a form to add exercises. Include fields for exercise name, sets, reps, weight, and optional notes. Each submission should insert into work out_exercises with the current session_id. Show a list of added exercises below the form. Provide a "Finish Workout" button to complete the session.

The resulting code will handle the relational inserts:

```
// Create session
const { data: session } = await supabase
  .from('workout_sessions')
  .insert({
    user_id: user.id,
    session_date: selectedDate,
    title: workoutTitle
  })
  .select()
  .single();
// Add exercise
await supabase
  .from('workout_exercises')
  .insert({
    session_id: session.id,
    exercise_name,
    sets,
    reps,
    weight,
    notes
  });
```

The previewed result is shown in Figure 8-2.

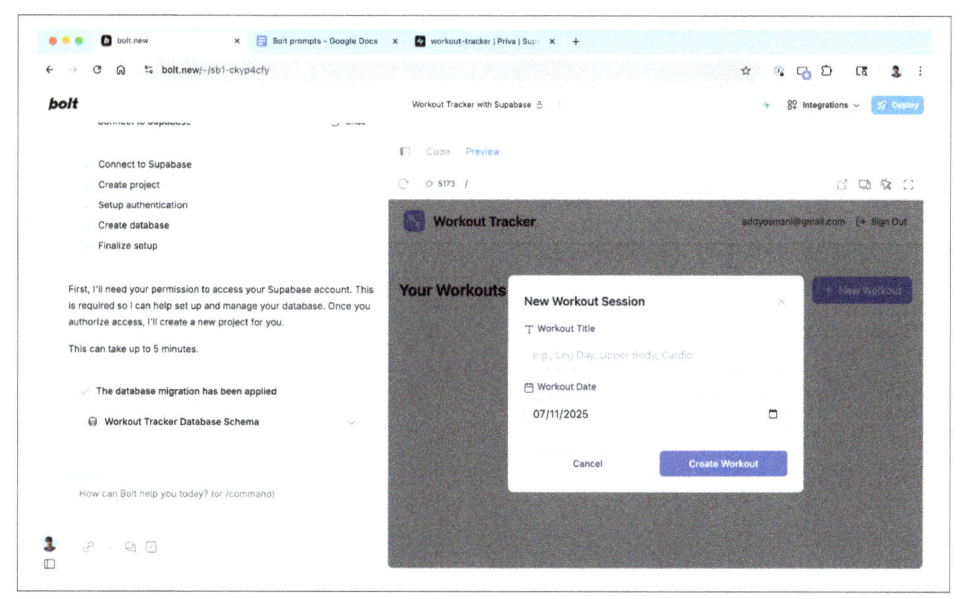

Figure 8-2. A modal for creating a new workout session with date and title entry

Displaying workout history

Next, prompt to show past workouts with their exercises:

Display a list of the user's workout sessions below the form. For each session, show the date, title, and all associated exercises with their sets × reps @ weight. Order sessions by date (newest first). Use a Supabase query that joins both tables.

Bolt will generate a query using Supabase's powerful `select` syntax:

```
const { data } = await supabase

  .from('workout_sessions')

  .select(`

    id,

    session_date,

    title,

    workout_exercises (

      id,

      exercise_name,
```

```
      sets,

      reps,

      weight,

      notes

    )

  `)

  .eq('user_id', user.id)

  .order('session_date', { ascending: false })

  .order('created_at', { ascending: false });
```

You can see the preview in Figure 8-3.

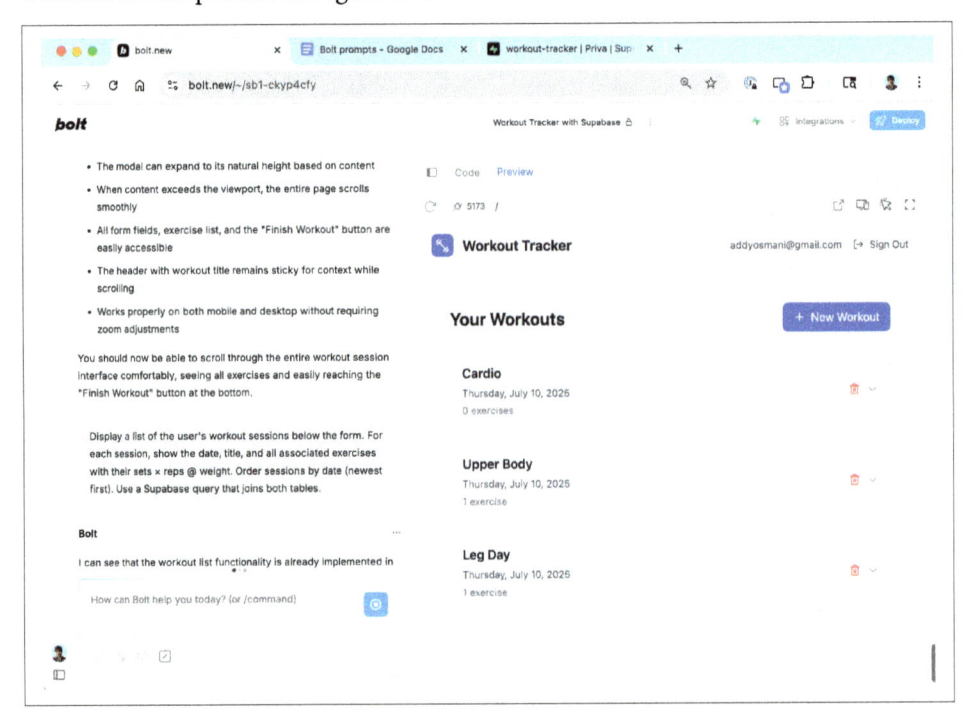

Figure 8-3. Workout Tracker app listing previously logged workout sessions

Deleting workouts

Next, prompt for deletion functionality:

> Add a delete button next to each workout session. When clicked, confirm with the user, then delete the session. The associated exercises should be automatically deleted due to the foreign key CASCADE setting. Refresh the list after deletion.

This feature is shown in preview in Figure 8-4.

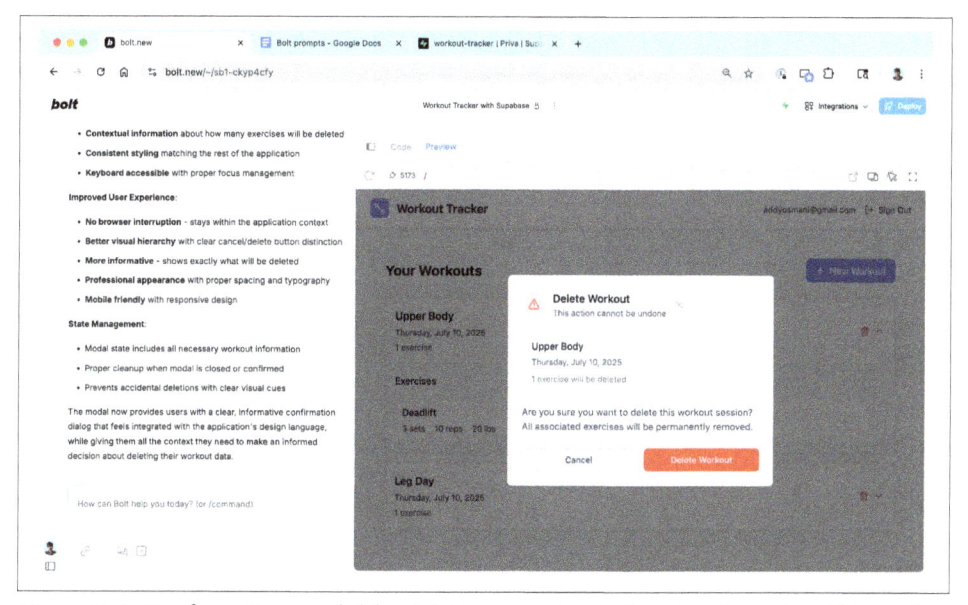

Figure 8-4. Confirmation modal for deleting a workout, showing clear visual hierarchy and context

Testing RLS

To test that RLS is working, create a few entries with one user account. Then create a second test account and use it to verify that the second user sees an empty workout list. Confirm that neither user can delete the other's workouts.

Understanding the Model-View-Controller (MVC) Pattern

This workout tracker beautifully demonstrates the MVC architecture pattern, pictured in Figure 8-5:

Model
> Our Supabase tables (`workout_sessions`, `workout_exercises`) and RLS policies handle data storage and business rules.

View

The React components render forms, lists, and UI elements.

Controller

Our Bolt-generated event handlers and hooks manage user input, call Supabase, and update the view.

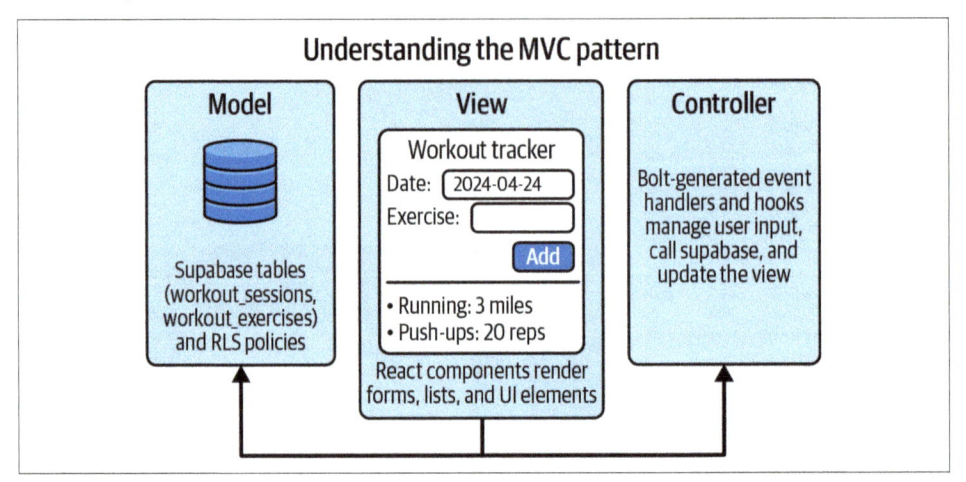

Figure 8-5. The Model-View-Controller (MVC) architecture pattern

MVC separates concerns, making code more maintainable and testable. In modern React apps, the View and Controller often blend together in components, while the Model remains clearly separated in the database layer.

Advanced Features (Optional)

The following features are optional but will enhance your app.

Real-time updates

Let's enable users to see live updates across multiple tabs or devices:

> Add real-time subscriptions to the workout data. When a workout is added, edited, or deleted, all connected clients should see the update immediately. Use Supabase's real-time features.

Bolt will implement code like the following:

```
useEffect(() => {

  const channel = supabase

    .channel('workout-changes')

    .on('postgres_changes', {
```

```
      event: '*',

      schema: 'public',

      table: 'workout_sessions',

      filter: `user_id=eq.${user.id}`

    }, payload => {

      // Refresh workout list

      fetchWorkouts();

    })

    .subscribe();

  return () => supabase.removeChannel(channel);

}, [user.id]);
```

Edge functions for server-side logic

Users often want to calculate their workout statistics. Supabase Edge Functions allow you to run backend code written in TypeScript or Deno in a geographically distributed network of servers (the "edge"). This means that when a user interacts with your application, the code they need to access runs closer to them, reducing latency and improving the app's responsiveness. As an example, let's prompt Bolt to create a function for weight lifting that calculates the user's total volume lifted:

> Create a Supabase Edge Function called `calculate-volume` that computes the total volume (sets × reps × weight) for a user's workouts. It should accept a date range and return the total volume lifted.

Here's an example of the kind of Edge Function it will generate:

```
import { serve } from 'https://deno.land/std/http/server.ts'

import { createClient } from 'https://esm.sh/@supabase/supabase-js@2'

serve(async (req) => {

  const supabase = createClient(

    Deno.env.get('SUPABASE_URL')!,

    Deno.env.get('SUPABASE_SERVICE_ROLE_KEY')!

  )
```

```
const { user_id, start_date, end_date } = await req.json()

const { data } = await supabase

  .from('workout_exercises')

  .select(`

   sets,

   reps,

   weight,

   workout_sessions!inner(user_id, session_date)

  `)

  .eq('workout_sessions.user_id', user_id)

  .gte('workout_sessions.session_date', start_date)

  .lte('workout_sessions.session_date', end_date)

 const totalVolume = data?.reduce((sum, exercise) =>

  sum + (exercise.sets * exercise.reps * exercise.weight), 0) || 0

 return new Response(JSON.stringify({ totalVolume }), {

  headers: { 'Content-Type': 'application/json' }

 })

})
```

Data visualization

Of course, it's not just statistics—people love to *see* their stats in charts and graphs, so let's add visual progress tracking:

> Add a chart showing workout frequency or total volume over time. Use Chart.js to create a line graph of workouts per week for the last 12 weeks. Include the chart at the top of the dashboard.

Bolt will install Chart.js and create a visualization component that processes your workout data into chart-friendly format.

Common Issues and Troubleshooting

Table 8-3 provides quick fixes for troubleshooting some of the most common issues.

Table 8-3. Troubleshooting the Supabase workout tracker

Issue	Cause	Solution
Insert failures	Missing `user_id` or RLS policy issues	Verify that `user_id` is included in inserts and RLS policies are correct.
Wrong sort order	Sorting by wrong field	Use `session_date` as the primary sort, with `created_at` as a tiebreaker.
Can't see data after login	RLS blocking access	Check that `user_id` matches `auth.uid()` in policies.
Exercises not deleting with session	Missing `CASCADE`	Ensure foreign key has `ON DELETE CASCADE`.
Date input issues	Format mismatch	Use the HTML date input type, which outputs in YYYY-MM-DD format.
Empty results for second user	Working as intended!	RLS is correctly isolating user data.

Best Practices

Building this workout tracker taught us several valuable lessons that apply to any data-driven application.

Start with the schema, not the UI

It's tempting to jump straight into building forms and buttons, but time spent planning your database structure pays dividends. Our two-table design might seem like overkill for a simple workout logger, but it elegantly handles the one-to-many relationship between sessions and exercises. This foundation makes it trivial to add features later. Want to track supersets? Add a `superset_id` field. Want workout templates? The structure already supports it. Good data design is like a good foundation for a house: it's invisible when done right, but everything depends on it.

Security isn't optional, even for hobby projects

The moment you enabled RLS, you transformed a vulnerable database into a secure one. RLS acts like a high-security vault with individual compartments. It doesn't matter if someone discovers your database URL and anon key (which are intentionally public): they still can't access data in compartments they're not authorized to open. Always enable RLS before inserting your first row of real data and test it with multiple user accounts. If user B can see user A's workouts, something's wrong with your policies.

Build vertically, not horizontally

Rather than creating all the forms, then all the displays, then all the delete buttons, build one complete feature at a time. Start with authentication: without that, nothing else matters. Then build one complete workflow: create a session, add an exercise, see it in the list. Only after this "vertical slice" works should you add the next feature. This approach gives you a deployable app at each step and makes debugging much easier.

Let the database do the heavy lifting

Supabase isn't just a storage bucket—it's a powerful PostgreSQL database. When you need sorted data, don't fetch everything and sort it in JavaScript. Let the database sort it. When you need to join sessions with exercises, use Supabase's relational query syntax rather than making multiple requests. The database is optimized for these operations and will always be faster than client-side manipulation. Plus, your code stays cleaner.

Remember that UI feedback is part of the feature, not an afterthought

When a user clicks "Save Workout," they need to know something happened. A loading spinner during the save, a success message after, and the new workout appearing in the list—these aren't nice-to-haves; they're essential for a professional feel. The same goes for error handling. When something fails (and it will), users need clear, actionable messages, not cryptic error codes. Bolt might not add these touches automatically, but a simple prompt like "add loading states and success messages" transforms a functional app into a polished one.

These practices aren't just for workout trackers. Whether you're building a task manager, a recipe book, or a social platform, the principles remain the same: design your data thoughtfully, secure it properly, build iteratively, leverage your database's power, and always keep the user informed. Master these, and you'll be building production-ready apps with Bolt in no time.

Summary

In this chapter, you built a full-featured workout tracker showcasing:

- Relational database design with proper foreign keys and constraints
- Row-level security (RLS), ensuring data privacy between users
- Complex forms handling multistep data entry
- Real-time capabilities for live updates (optional)
- Server-side logic with Edge Functions (optional)
- Data visualization for progress tracking (optional)

The app demonstrates how Bolt can generate production-ready code for data-intensive applications. With Supabase handling the backend complexity and Bolt scaffolding the frontend, you've created a secure, scalable fitness tracking application with minimal manual coding.

Deploy this app to Netlify just like the Movie Explorer—the process is identical. Your Supabase keys are safe to include in the client code because RLS protects the actual data.

Next, in Chapter 9, you'll explore a different side of Bolt: converting Figma designs directly into working code. Instead of focusing on data and logic, you'll see how Bolt handles visual design and styling, turning mockups into interactive applications.

CHAPTER 9

Building a Grocery List App Using Bolt's Figma Integration

In this chapter, we'll explore Bolt's integration with Figma, a popular UI design tool, to build a simple grocery list app.

Modern product-development teams rarely start with code. Instead, they begin in design tools like Figma, crafting pixel-perfect interfaces before writing a single line of JavaScript. This chapter explores that workflow through a practical project: building a mobile-first grocery list application that bridges the gap between visual design and functional code.

We'll start by creating a simple interface in Figma, then use Bolt's integration to transform that static design into a working React application. Along the way, you'll learn how design decisions impact code generation, why certain Figma features produce cleaner output, and how to layer interactivity onto an imported interface.

Understanding the Design-to-Code Pipeline

Before we dive into building, let's understand what happens when you click "Import from Figma" in Bolt. Behind the scenes, Bolt uses technology from Anima, a platform that specializes in translating visual designs into production-ready code. Anima reads your Figma file's structure—the frames, typography, spacing, and, most importantly, the auto layout settings—and generates corresponding HTML, CSS, and React components.

This isn't magic, though it can feel like it. Anima looks for patterns in your design that map to common web development patterns. A vertically stacked set of frames with consistent spacing becomes a flexbox container. Repeated elements with similar structure become reusable components. Text layers become semantic HTML elements. The cleaner and more structured your design, the cleaner the generated code.

Setting Up Your Design Environment

You'll need a Figma account (*https://figma.com/signup*) for this chapter. The free tier (*https://figma.com/pricing*) provides everything necessary for our grocery list project. Head to *figma.com* and create an account if you haven't already. While you're there, familiarize yourself with the interface: the layers panel (*https://oreil.ly/m45oZ*) on the left, the design canvas in the center, and the properties panel on the right will be your primary tools.

For the fastest path through this chapter, you can download a premade Figma file from this book's repository (*https://bolt.addy.ie*). It already incorporates the best practices we'll discuss, so your import experience will match what I describe. However, building the design yourself offers valuable insights into how design decisions affect code generation.

Project Requirements

Here's what we want the grocery list app to let users do:

- View a list of grocery items.
- Add new items via an input field.
- Check items off the list.
- Remove items from the list.

This means its design elements should include:

- A header: Grocery List
- A scrollable list area (with some sample items, like Apples and Bread)
- A checkbox next to each item to toggle between complete and incomplete statuses
- A strikethrough on each item when it's marked as completed
- An input field at the bottom with placeholder text "Add new item…" and an Add button or plus icon

Creating the Grocery List Design

Let's build our interface from scratch. Open Figma and create a new design file (*https://oreil.ly/mPVYi*). We'll design for mobile first, since grocery lists are primarily used on phones, but we'll structure it to be responsive from the start.

Press F to activate the Frame tool (*https://oreil.ly/H8gNe*). In the right sidebar, you'll see device presets (*https://oreil.ly/NrmwI*). Choose iPhone or a similar mobile frame. This gives us realistic constraints to work within. Name your frame GroceryList-Mobile by double-clicking its name in the layers panel. Meaningful names aren't just for organization—they become component names in your generated code.

Now comes the most critical step: enabling auto layout (*https://oreil.ly/lzrZy*). Select your frame and press Shift+A, or find the auto layout section in the right panel and click the plus icon. Set the direction to vertical. This single action transforms your static frame into a flexible container that behaves like a CSS flexbox (*https://oreil.ly/FU9zy*). Without auto layout, Anima might generate absolute positioning that breaks on different screen sizes. With it, you get responsive code from the start.

Inside your auto layout frame, let's build our interface components. Start with the header. Use the Text tool (T) (*https://oreil.ly/Ua6t9*) to create a title that reads Grocery List. In the layers panel, rename this text layer to HeaderTitle. Set the font size to 24 pixels and make it bold. The specific font doesn't matter much, but system fonts like SF Pro and Inter translate more reliably than custom fonts.

Next, we'll create a reusable list item component. This is where thoughtful design pays dividends. Create a new frame using the Frame tool (F) and name it ListItem. Enable auto layout on this frame with horizontal direction. Inside, add three elements:

- Create a checkbox. You can draw a 20 × 20 pixel square with the Rectangle tool (R) (*https://oreil.ly/TQJQA*) and add a checkmark shape inside, or search Figma's community resources for a checkbox component. Name it ItemCheckbox.

- Add item text using the Text tool. Type Sample Item as placeholder text and name the layer ItemText. Set the font size to 16 pixels.

- Create a delete button. For simplicity, use the Text tool to add an X character, styled in red. Name this DeleteButton. You could use an icon instead, but text requires no external assets.

Select all three elements and ensure they're properly spaced within your ListItem auto layout frame. Set the gap between elements to 12 pixels. This creates visual breathing room that will translate to proper spacing in CSS.

Now duplicate your ListItem frame a few times to simulate a list. Change the text in each to common grocery items like Milk, Eggs, and Bread. Check one or two checkboxes and apply a strikethrough text style to simulate completed items. These visual states help Anima understand the intended interactivity.

At the bottom of your main frame, create the input area. Draw a rectangle for the text input field, roughly 240 pixels wide and 40 pixels tall. Add placeholder text on top that reads "Add new item…" and group these together as InputField. Next to it, create an Add button—another rectangle with text inside. Group this as AddButton.

Select both the InputField and AddButton groups and apply auto layout with horizontal direction. Name this container AddItemForm. This structure tells Anima these elements work together as a unit.

Your layers panel should now show a clear hierarchy (Figure 9-1): GroceryList-Mobile contains HeaderTitle, several ListItem instances, and AddItemForm. This organization directly influences the component structure in your generated code.

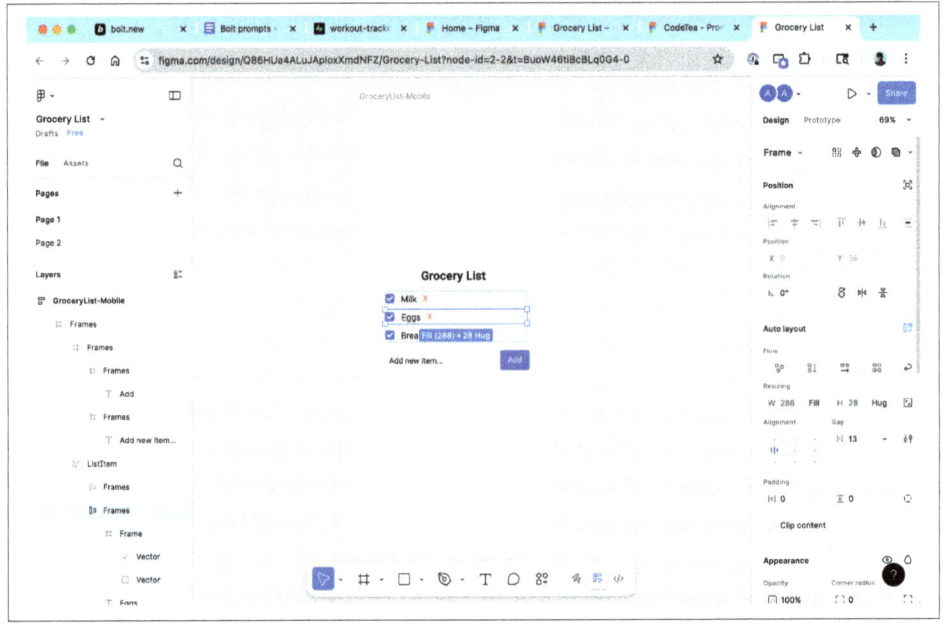

Figure 9-1. Figma design of a grocery list app with checkboxes and delete buttons

Preparing for Export

Before importing to Bolt, let's ensure our design follows best practices that lead to cleaner code generation. Double-check that every meaningful element has a descriptive name. Generic names like "Frame 1" or "Text" become unhelpful variable names in code.

Verify that auto layout is applied consistently. The main frame should use vertical auto layout, each ListItem should use horizontal auto layout, and the AddItemForm should also use horizontal auto layout. These nested layouts translate to nested flexbox containers in CSS, creating naturally responsive designs.

Consider your color choices. If you've used the same blue for the Add button and checkmarks, Anima might recognize this pattern and create a CSS variable. Consistent spacing also helps (Figure 9-2). If you use 16 pixels between all major sections, this might become a spacing token in the generated code.

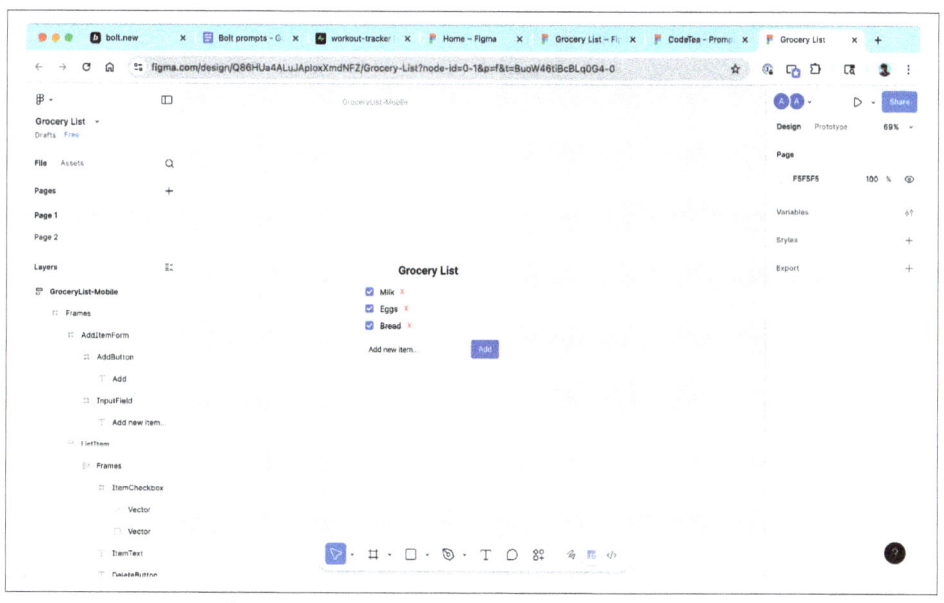

Figure 9-2. Improved spacing and alignment in the grocery list design in Figma

Importing into Bolt

With your design complete, it's time to bridge into code (*https://oreil.ly/cHpj0*). In Figma, select your main frame and click the Share button in the top toolbar. Choose "Copy link" from the drop-down (Figure 9-3). Don't use "Copy prototype link." We want the design view, not the presentation view.

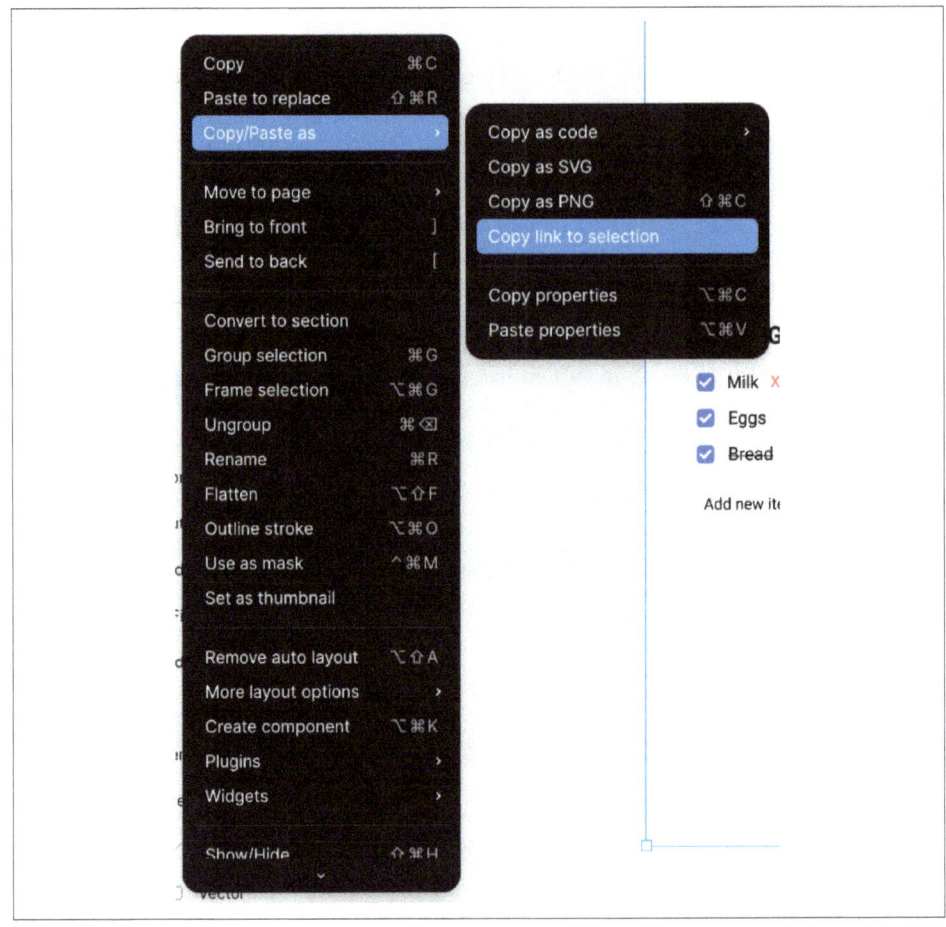

Figure 9-3. Copying the frame link from Figma

Next, you'll need to connect your Bolt account to your Figma account (Figures 9-4 and 9-5). On Bolt, go to Settings → Applications, find Figma, and click Connect. It will ask for your Figma login and permission. Authorize it.

Open Bolt and create a new project. You'll see an option to "Import from Figma" on the project creation screen. Click it and paste your Figma link (Figure 9-6). Bolt connects to Anima's service, analyzes your design, and generates a React project.

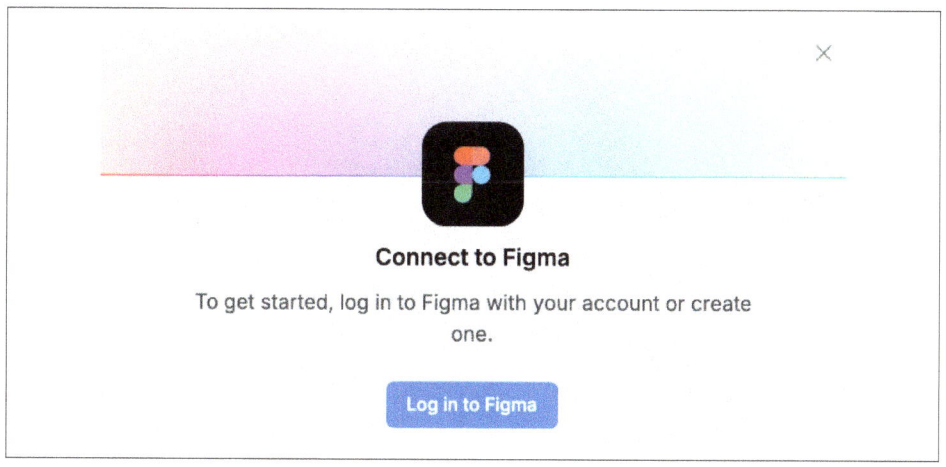

Figure 9-4. Connecting Bolt to Figma

bolt

Bolt.new would like to access your account and be able to:

- ✓ Read the contents of files you can access
- ✓ Read comments for files you can access
- ✓ List projects and files you can access
- ✓ Read components and styles you can access
- ✓ Read your name, email, and profile image

Allow access

Logged in as addyosmani@gmail.com.

Switch accounts

Figure 9-5. Bolt connecting to Figma using OAuth permissions dialog

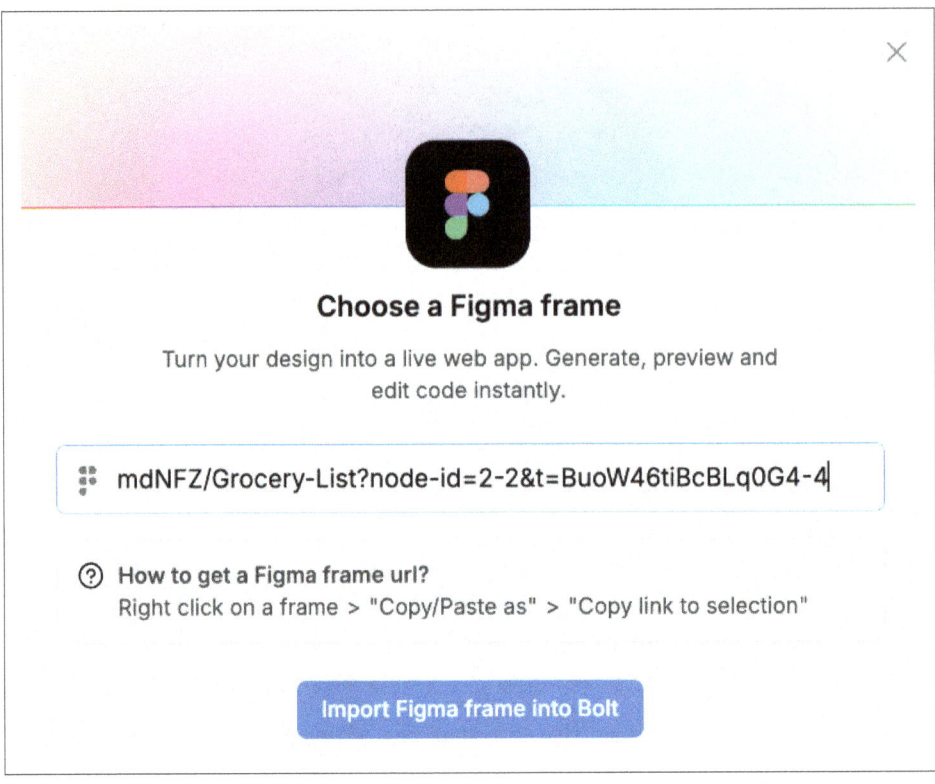

Figure 9-6. Entering a Figma frame link to begin code generation in Bolt

The import process typically takes 10 to 30 seconds. When complete, Bolt opens an editor showing your generated code. Take a moment to explore the file structure. You'll likely see an *App.js* file containing your main component, possibly separate component files for repeated elements like ListItem, and CSS files with your styling (Figure 9-7).

The generated code reflects your design decisions. If you've used auto layout consistently, you'll see flexbox CSS. If you've named your layers well, you'll see meaningful component and variable names. The static list items from your design appear as hardcoded JSX elements. Our next task is making them dynamic.

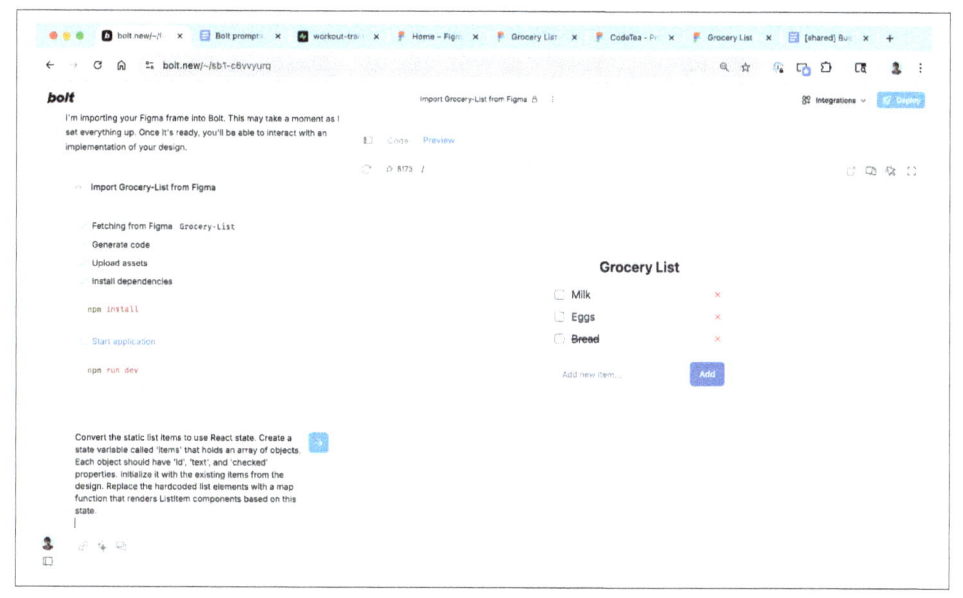

Figure 9-7. Preview of the initial version of the generated grocery list app after import

From Static Design to Dynamic Application

The imported code provides structure but lacks behavior. Our grocery list currently displays the same items forever, and clicking buttons does nothing. Let's fix that by introducing React's state management (*https://oreil.ly/sRJ4R*).

Understanding state is crucial for what comes next. In React, state represents data that can change over time. When state changes, React automatically updates the user interface to reflect the new data. For our grocery list, the items themselves are state—they can be added, removed, or marked complete.

Let's start by making the list dynamic. Currently, your code probably contains something like hardcoded list items. We need to replace these with items generated from a state array. Create your first Bolt prompt:

> Convert the static list items to use React state. Create a state variable called "items" that holds an array of objects. Each object should have "id," "text," and "checked" properties. Initialize it with the existing items from the design. Replace the hardcoded list elements with a map function that renders ListItem components based on this state.

Bolt will modify your code to include React's `useState` hook. This hook creates a state variable and a function to update it. The syntax might look unfamiliar if you're new to React, but think of it as creating a special variable that triggers UI updates when changed.

The map function that Bolt adds is JavaScript's way of transforming arrays. It takes each item object and returns a ListItem component, creating a dynamic list that always reflects the current state. Notice how Bolt adds a "key" prop to each mapped item—React uses these keys to efficiently update the list when items change.

Adding Interactivity

With our list now driven by state, we can add the ability to create new items. The input field and Add button need to work together: the input tracks what the user types, and the button adds that text as a new item. Prompt Bolt:

> Make the Add Item form functional. Track the input field's value in state. When the Add button is clicked or Enter is pressed in the input, create a new item with a unique ID and add it to the items array. Clear the input after adding. Don't add empty items.

Bolt implements this with another useState hook (*https://oreil.ly/-t0VN*) for the input value. It also adds event handlers (*https://oreil.ly/cITfQ*), functions that run in response to user actions. The onChange handler (*https://oreil.ly/7ksTw*) updates the input state with each keystroke, creating what React calls a "controlled component," where React explicitly manages the input's value.

The Add button gets an onClick handler that constructs a new item object and adds it to the array. Bolt likely uses the spread operator (...items) to create a new array rather than modifying the existing one—this immutable update pattern is crucial for React to detect state changes.

Test your progress: type "Cheese" and click Add. The new item should appear immediately. Try adding an empty item—nothing should happen. Try pressing Enter in the input field—it should work just like clicking Add.

Implementing Checkbox Functionality

Our checkboxes look interactive but don't actually work yet. Let's connect them to state changes:

> When a checkbox is clicked, toggle that item's checked property in state. Apply a strikethrough style to checked items. Make sure the checkbox visual state reflects the checked property.

Bolt adds an onChange handler to each checkbox that finds the corresponding item and flips its checked value. The style update might use conditional CSS classes or inline styles. Either approach works, but classes are generally cleaner.

The key insight here is that we never modify the items array directly. Instead, we create a new array with the updated item, maintaining React's expectation of immutable updates. This pattern appears throughout React applications. Always create new objects or arrays rather than modifying existing ones.

Enabling Item Deletion

The X buttons need to remove items from our list. This is simpler than toggling—we just filter out the deleted item:

> When the delete button (X) is clicked, remove that item from the items array. Use the filter method to create a new array excluding the deleted item.

The filter method is perfect for this task. It creates a new array containing only items that pass a test. In our case, the test is "is this not the item we're deleting?" Bolt implements this with a comparison using the item's ID.

Test the complete flow (Figure 9-8): add several items, check some off, delete others. The list should update smoothly with each action. If items disappear or the wrong item gets deleted, the issue likely lies in how IDs are being compared.

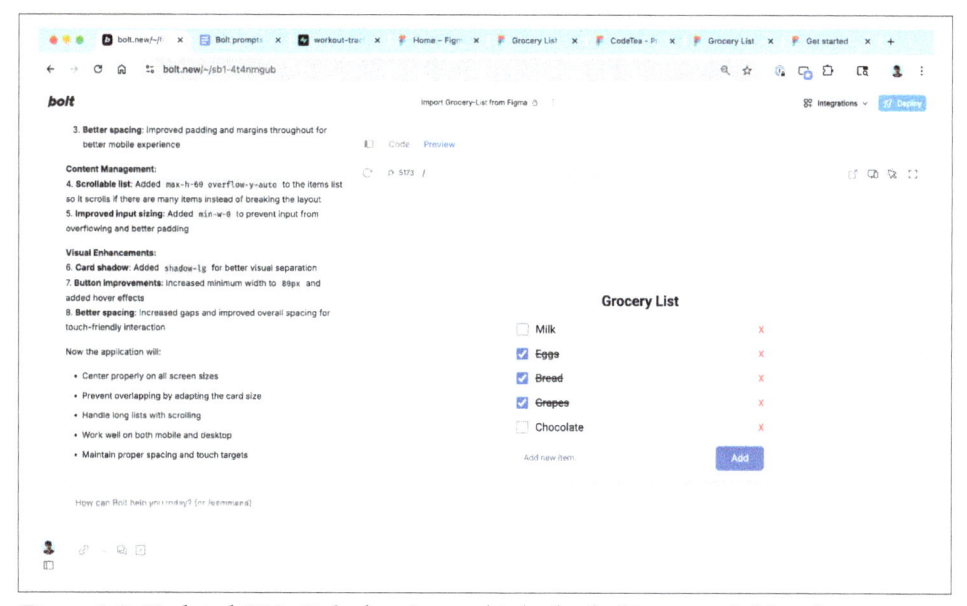

Figure 9-8. Updated UI in Bolt showing multiple checked items and delete buttons

Adding Persistence

Currently, refreshing the page wipes out your grocery list. Browser `localStorage` (*https://oreil.ly/CDpAe*) provides a simple solution. It's a key-value store that persists data even after closing the browser. Let's prompt:

> Save the items array to localStorage whenever it changes. When the app loads, check localStorage for saved items and use them as the initial state. Store the data as a JSON string.

Bolt implements this with React's useEffect hook (*https://oreil.ly/r8Tqs*). This hook handles "side effects"—operations that interact with the world outside React. One effect loads saved items when the component mounts. Another effect saves items whenever they change.

The dependency array in useEffect is crucial. An empty array means "run once when mounting." An array with [items] means "run whenever items changes." This declarative approach eliminates the need to manually track when to save or load data.

Test persistence by adding items, refreshing the page, and confirming they remain. Open your browser's developer tools to see the actual localStorage data. In Chrome, find the Application tab and look under Local Storage.

Enhancing Responsiveness

While our Figma auto layout provides basic responsiveness, we can enhance it further. The Add button and input field might need to stack on very narrow screens, so let's prompt:

> Ensure the AddItemForm responds well to narrow screens. On mobile widths, if the button and input don't fit side by side, stack them vertically. The input should stretch to fill available width while the button maintains a reasonable minimum width.

Bolt might add media queries or rely on flexbox's natural wrapping behavior. The key is avoiding fixed pixel widths where percentages or flex properties work better. The input field might use flex: 1 to fill available space, while the button uses flex: 0 0 auto to maintain its natural size.

Polishing the User Experience

Small details elevate good apps to great ones. Let's add two refinements that make the app feel more professional.

First, after adding an item, users shouldn't need to click back into the input field. We can automatically restore focus:

> After successfully adding an item, automatically focus the input field so users can immediately type the next item. Use a ref to access the input element directly.

React refs (*https://oreil.ly/_m1T2*) provide direct access to DOM elements. While React usually manages the DOM for us, sometimes we need to imperatively control focus, scroll position, or other browser APIs. The inputRef.current.focus() call tells the browser to make our input the active element.

Second, let's make the list area scrollable if it grows too long:

Make the list area scrollable when it contains many items. The header and add form should remain visible while the list scrolls. Set a reasonable maximum height for the list container.

This involves CSS more than React. Bolt might add `overflow-y: auto` to the list container and set a `max-height`. The exact implementation depends on your layout structure, but the goal is keeping critical controls always accessible.

Common Issues and Troubleshooting

Several issues commonly arise when working with Figma imports. Understanding them helps you debug problems and design better from the start.

Absolute positioning
Absolute positioning often appears when Figma frames lack auto layout. The generated code might position elements with exact pixel coordinates, breaking responsiveness. The fix involves either updating the Figma design or prompting Bolt to rebuild with flexbox.

Generic naming
Generic naming in Figma leads to unclear code. A component named "Frame 42" becomes an unhelpful variable name. While you can rename things after import, starting with clear names saves time and reduces confusion.

State update patterns
State update patterns cause subtle bugs. If items don't update correctly, check whether state is being mutated directly rather than replaced. React only rerenders when state is replaced with new objects or arrays, not when existing ones are modified.

Cross-origin issues
Cross-origin issues affect external images. If your Figma design includes images hosted elsewhere, browser security policies might block them. Use inline SVGs or text-based icons to avoid this entirely.

Design Patterns for Better Imports

Through experience, I've found that certain Figma patterns consistently produce better code. Mastering these patterns streamlines your workflow and reduces post-import cleanup.

Component instances in Figma translate well to React components. If you create a component for ListItem in Figma and use instances of it, Anima is more likely to generate a reusable React component rather than duplicated code.

Consistent spacing creates cleaner CSS. If you use 16 pixels between all major sections, Anima might recognize this pattern and create a spacing variable. Random spacing values lead to magic numbers scattered throughout your CSS.

Semantic color usage improves maintainability. Using the same color for all interactive elements (buttons, links, checkboxes) might result in a CSS variable like `--primary-color`. This makes theme changes trivial.

Auto layout constraints determine responsive behavior. Elements set to "Fill container" become `flex: 1`. Elements set to "Fixed width" maintain their size. Understanding these mappings helps you design with the generated code in mind.

Extending Beyond the Basics

Our grocery list is intentionally simple, but the patterns we've explored can also scale to complex applications. The same workflow—design in Figma, import to Bolt, add interactivity through prompts—works for dashboards, social feeds, or ecommerce interfaces.

Consider how you might extend this app. Categories could organize items by store section. Quantities could track how much to buy. Sharing could let family members collaborate on one list. Each feature follows the same pattern: design the UI, import it, then add behavior through React state and effects.

The Figma integration especially shines when designers and developers collaborate. Designers can focus on visual excellence, while developers add logic and data flow. The generated code provides a common ground, reducing miscommunication and repeated work.

Summary

This chapter demonstrated a fundamentally different approach from our previous projects. Instead of describing an interface through prompts, we drew it visually and let tools translate that vision to code. This workflow mirrors professional development teams where design precedes implementation.

There are key insights worth remembering. First, good design practices in Figma directly impact code quality. Auto layout, semantic naming, and component reuse aren't just design niceties—they determine whether your generated code is maintainable or chaotic.

Second, the import gets you started, not finished. Expecting pixel-perfect, fully interactive applications from a static design import isn't realistic. Instead, view it as accelerating the most tedious part of development: translating a visual design into structured markup and styles.

Third, React patterns remain consistent regardless of how you start. Whether you begin with a Figma import or an empty file, you'll use state for dynamic data, effects for side effects, and refs for imperative operations. The import just provides a different starting point.

Our simple grocery list required no backend, no authentication, and no complex state management. Yet it's a fully functional application that looks professional and works reliably. Sometimes the simplest solutions are the best ones. In our next chapter, we'll explore Bolt's integration with StackBlitz.

CHAPTER 10

StackBlitz for Bolt Users

In this chapter, we'll work with the Movie Explorer app you built in Chapters 5 and 6. Now you're ready to take manual control of your project by transitioning your Bolt project into the StackBlitz editor (both are products from the StackBlitz company). We'll start with the basics of StackBlitz, then walk step by step through exporting your project and developing in the cloud editor. You'll get a feel for the workflow differences between Bolt's AI-driven approach and hands-on coding with StackBlitz. By the time we're done enhancing your TMDB movie app with new features, you'll be comfortable using StackBlitz as both a powerful tutorial platform and a daily development environment.

Before we dive in, let's set clear expectations. Using StackBlitz means you'll be editing code directly rather than describing changes in natural language. You'll need basic familiarity with the programming language your app uses—likely JavaScript or TypeScript, along with HTML and CSS—or at least be willing to learn by examining and modifying the code that Bolt generated. This isn't a "no-code" experience anymore; it's where you transition from AI-assisted development to hands-on programming. Don't worry if you're not an expert: Bolt gave you a solid starting point, and you can learn tremendously by experimenting with the code it created. However, if you've never seen a line of JavaScript before, you might want to spend some time with a basic programming tutorial before jumping into StackBlitz.

While you can use StackBlitz without an account, I strongly recommend creating a free StackBlitz account before you begin. You can sign up directly on *stackblitz.com* or log in using an existing GitHub or Google account. Having an account ensures you can save your work, return to projects later, and access additional features like GitHub integration. If you're using StackBlitz through an educational platform like O'Reilly, an account might be created automatically when you first open the editor, but it's still worth verifying that you can access your projects later.

StackBlitz Overview

StackBlitz (*https://oreil.ly/ZdZKQ*) is an online *integrated development environment* (IDE) that runs entirely in your web browser. Think of it as Google Docs for coding: you can create, edit, and run code instantly online without installing anything on your computer. There's no need to set up a local development server, install Node.js, or configure build tools—StackBlitz handles all of that behind the scenes. You simply open StackBlitz, choose a project template (like Angular, React, or plain JavaScript), and you're immediately ready to code with a fully functional development environment. Because everything runs in the cloud, you avoid the common developer frustration of "it works on my machine" problems. Every person who opens your project sees it running in exactly the same environment.

StackBlitz accomplishes this through a technology called WebContainers (*https://webcontainers.io*), which allows Node.js code to run inside your browser. To understand how remarkable this is, consider that traditionally, running server-side code required either a separate server or your local machine. WebContainers represent a breakthrough that essentially puts a tiny Node.js-enabled computer inside your browser tab. This technology, pioneered by StackBlitz (*https://oreil.ly/Xtztc*) in 2021, uses WebAssembly to create what you might think of as a lightweight operating system that can execute Node.js applications entirely within the browser's security sandbox.

The practical benefits of this approach are transformative for development:

- You can run `npm install` to add packages right in the browser, just as you would on your local machine. The packages are fetched and installed within the WebContainer environment, becoming immediately available for use in your code.

- You can start up an Express server (as you did in Chapter 5) and it truly runs, serving HTTP requests and handling backend logic, all without leaving the browser. The server operates within the WebContainer and can be accessed through special URLs that StackBlitz generates.

- The environment boots up extremely fast and consistently every time. Unlike traditional development setups that can break or behave differently across machines, WebContainers provide identical environments for everyone.

- Everything runs securely and isolated within your browser's sandbox. The code isn't actually installing things on your physical machine, so it can't harm your system or access your personal files. This isolation gives you complete freedom to experiment with packages and configurations without any risk to your computer.

When Bolt creates your project, its AI agent operates within this same WebContainer environment with special privileges. The AI isn't just writing code—it's actually controlling the filesystem, running terminal commands, and starting servers within the container. That's why, when you ask Bolt for a Next.js app, it can immediately initialize the project (running `npm install` and `npm run dev` internally) and show you a working application with a live development server. All of this complex setup happens automatically in the WebContainer, and you see the result in Bolt's preview pane.

Think of WebContainers as a "container ship in a bottle": a full container environment like Docker, shrunk down to fit inside the confines of a web browser. It's an engineering marvel that enables remarkable capabilities. For example, you could prompt Bolt:

> Set up a new Express.js route at /api/users that returns a JSON list of users.

Bolt will create a server file (if it's not already present) and add that route. The server will run in the WebContainer, and you can actually access that */api/users* URL from the browser preview. The response comes straight from the in-browser Node server, running at a URL like *https://<project-id>.webcontainer.io/api/users*.

When you use external services like Supabase with Bolt, while the database itself doesn't run in the WebContainer (Supabase is a cloud service), any code to query or authenticate runs in your Bolt app's Node environment within the container. This means you could have server routes that query Supabase, call Stripe APIs, or interact with any external service, and it all executes securely within your browser sandbox.

You might wonder, "I already built my app with Bolt's help. Why do I need StackBlitz?" The answer lies in the progression from assisted development to independent coding. Bolt excels at rapidly generating projects through AI guidance, but as your skills develop and your project requirements become more specific, you'll want granular control over every aspect of your code. StackBlitz provides that detailed control in an accessible environment.

Using Bolt is like having an expert driver handle your car while you give directions about where you want to go. The AI handles the technical mechanics of coding while you focus on describing your desired outcomes. StackBlitz is like taking the wheel yourself. You're responsible for the steering, acceleration, and navigation, but you have complete control over the route and can make precise adjustments based on the road conditions you observe.

For developers with limited experience, StackBlitz removes the intimidating setup barriers that often prevent people from learning to code. You won't need to configure webpack, install Node.js versions, or troubleshoot environment conflicts during this learning phase. Instead, you can focus entirely on understanding how code works by directly modifying it and observing immediate results. The interface is visual and interactive, helping you build mental connections between the code you write and the behavior you see in your running application.

In essence, StackBlitz provides a complete full stack development environment accessible through any modern web browser. For someone transitioning from Bolt, this means you can evolve from AI-generated starting points to hands-on programming without needing to install or configure anything new on your computer.

Exporting Your Bolt Project to StackBlitz

Bolt's creators designed the platform knowing that users would eventually want to refine their AI-generated projects manually. That's why Bolt provides a straightforward way to open your project directly in StackBlitz. Here's the step-by-step process:

1. *Open your Bolt project.*

   Launch Bolt and navigate to the Movie Explorer app you created in earlier chapters. You should see the familiar Bolt interface with your app preview displayed alongside the AI chat history where you guided the development process.

2. *Locate the export option.*

   Look for your project name at the top of the Bolt interface. Next to it, you'll find a drop-down menu. Click this menu and select Export, then choose Open in StackBlitz. This option appears with a distinctive lightning-bolt icon ⚡ that represents StackBlitz's branding, as shown in Figure 10-1.

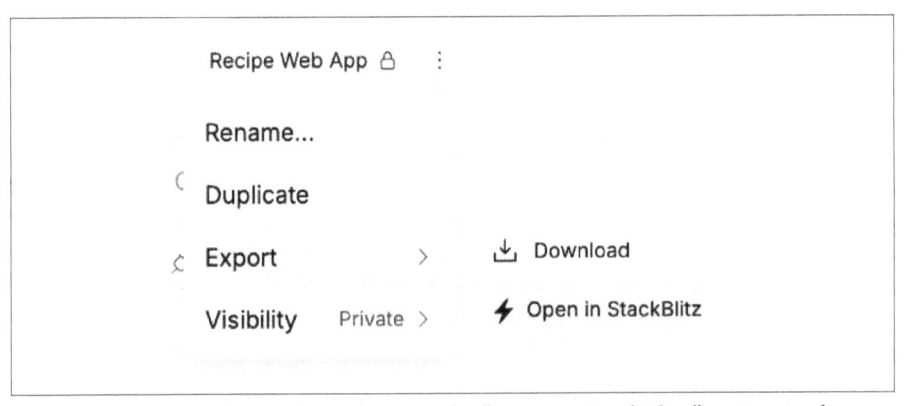

Figure 10-1. The Bolt interface, showing the "Open in StackBlitz" option in the project menu

3. *Initiate the export process.*

   When you click Open in StackBlitz, Bolt packages your entire project—all the code files, dependencies, configuration, and even environment variables—and transfers it to StackBlitz. This action typically opens a new browser tab or window that loads the StackBlitz editor. You might see a loading indicator for several seconds as StackBlitz sets up the WebContainer environment, installs your project's dependencies, and starts the development server.

4. *Handle account requirements.*

When StackBlitz opens, you may be prompted to sign in, or you might find that an account has been created automatically (particularly if you're accessing Stack-Blitz through an educational platform). If you see your project running under a randomly generated username, you're essentially working anonymously. While this works fine for immediate experimentation, sign in with your preferred method (GitHub, Google, or email) to ensure you can save your work and access it later. Some integrations, like O'Reilly's platform, automatically create a free StackBlitz account tied to your email address when you first launch the editor.

5. *Let the project load completely.*

Once StackBlitz finishes setting up, you should see your project's complete code structure in the editor. The interface includes a file explorer showing all your project files, a code editor in the center, and a live preview of your running application. StackBlitz automatically installs all dependencies listed in your *package.json* file and starts the development server. Bolt assigns a default name to your project during export, but you can rename it within StackBlitz by clicking on the project name.

6. *Verify full functionality.*

StackBlitz automatically runs projects when they load, so your Movie Explorer app should appear in the preview pane and be fully interactive. Take time to thoroughly test the application. If your app includes features like movie search, detailed views, or API integrations, test each of these functions to ensure everything works exactly as it did in Bolt. Since the code is identical and the WebContainer environment is similar to Bolt's backend, functionality should be preserved seamlessly.

The export process handles most complexities automatically, but occasionally you might encounter issues. If some images don't load, the app doesn't respond properly, or API calls fail, first verify that Bolt completely finished generating your project before export. Check whether any API keys or environment variables need to be reconfigured in the new environment—these should transfer automatically, but sometimes manual verification is needed. In most cases, the "Open in StackBlitz" button handles everything for you.

 If you ever lose track of your project, you can always repeat the export process from Bolt to StackBlitz. Also, while in StackBlitz, click Save to store the project to your StackBlitz account. This way, you can easily find it from your StackBlitz dashboard later without going through Bolt again.

Now that your project is live in StackBlitz, it's time to get comfortable with the StackBlitz development environment. In the next section, we'll tour the StackBlitz editor so you can learn how to navigate files, edit code, and see your results in real time.

Developing in the StackBlitz Cloud Editor

This section will cover how to navigate your files, make code changes, and observe the results instantly within the StackBlitz cloud editor.

The StackBlitz Interface Tour

When you first look at the StackBlitz editor, it might seem similar to other code editors or IDEs you've seen (it has a layout reminiscent of Visual Studio Code, see Figure 10-2).

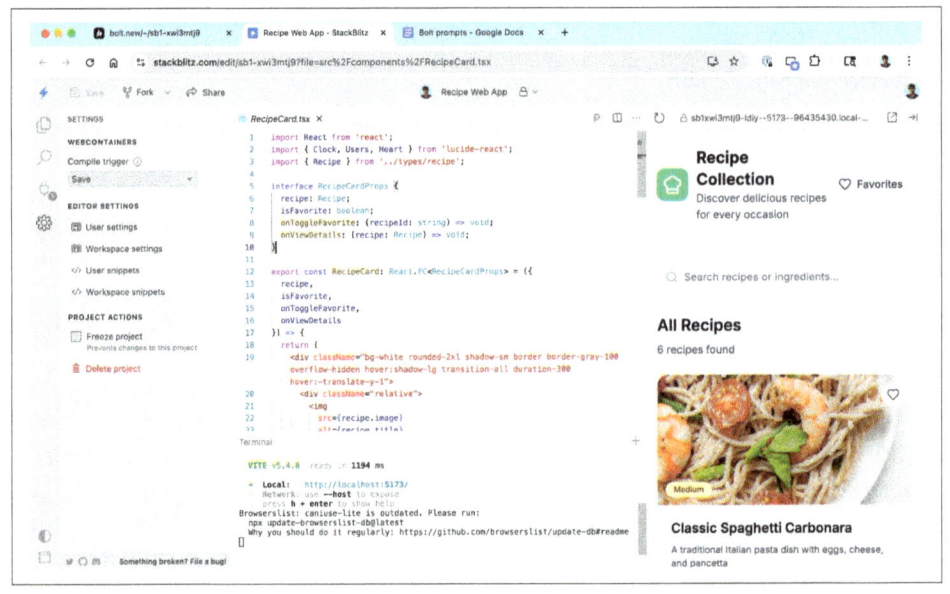

Figure 10-2. The StackBlitz editor, showing the file explorer on the left, the code editor in the middle, the terminal pane on the bottom, and a live preview of the app on the right

Here's a breakdown of the main parts of the interface:

File explorer (project tree)
On the left side, you'll see a panel listing all the files and folders in your project, providing complete transparency into the structure that Bolt created. This is where you can browse and open different files (HTML, JavaScript/TypeScript, CSS). For your Movie Explorer app, you might see files like *index.html*, some source code files (perhaps *app.js* or *main.ts*, depending on the framework), and a *package.json* file (which lists your dependencies—the libraries your app uses). This visibility into the full project structure is one of the key differences from Bolt's more abstracted interface—you can now see exactly how your application is organized and where each piece of functionality lives.

Editor pane
In the center is the code editor, where you'll spend most of your development time. When you click a file from the explorer, it opens in this pane with comprehensive syntax highlighting that color-codes different parts of the code to improve readability. The editor supports professional-grade features including auto-indentation, bracket matching, code folding, and multi-cursor editing. You can click anywhere in the code to start editing—it's just like using a desktop code editor, except it runs entirely in your browser. If you're editing JavaScript or TypeScript files, you might also get intelligent autocompletion suggestions as you type, especially if you've enabled AI coding assistants or StackBlitz's built-in suggestions.

Preview pane
StackBlitz typically shows a live preview of your running application on the right side (or sometimes as a separate tab within the interface). You'll see your Movie Explorer app's UI here in what's essentially a mini web browser inside StackBlitz. If your project is an Angular or React app, StackBlitz runs the development server in the background and displays the result here. The preview updates automatically whenever your code changes thanks to hot reload functionality. If the preview area feels too small, you can open it in a new window using the "Open in New Window" button above the preview, popping the app out into a full browser tab for a larger view.

Console/terminal panel
Below the editor (or sometimes below the preview), there's a multipurpose panel that serves both as a runtime console and a command-line terminal. In console mode, it displays runtime messages from your application—any `con sole.log("Fetching movies...")` statements in your code will appear here, along with error messages and warnings. If an error occurs (say you try to call a function that doesn't exist), the error stack trace will show up in this panel. StackBlitz captures this output automatically, so you don't need to open the

browser's developer console separately (though you can still do that for more advanced debugging). There's usually a toggle or tab to switch between a Console view (showing logs) and a Terminal view (where you can type commands).

Toolbar and menu

At the top of the editor, StackBlitz has a comprehensive menu bar with several useful controls. You'll find the project's name (which you can click to rename it) and buttons to Save, Fork, and Share the project. If you're logged in and own the project, you'll also see options to Connect to GitHub or a Commit button for version control (more on that in the GitHub section). There's also a profile avatar (if you're logged in) and a project visibility indicator (public, private, or secret). On the left side of the toolbar or sidebar, there may be icons to toggle various side panels: a Project icon (to show/hide the file explorer), a Search icon (to search within files), a Ports icon (to view any open ports your app uses, relevant for backend processes), and a Settings icon (to adjust editor settings and project options).

"Ask Bolt.new" integration

You might notice a small chat icon or a box labeled Ask Bolt (or Ask Bolt.new) in the interface (often in the bottom-left corner or as a sidebar tab). This indicates that StackBlitz has built-in integration with Bolt's AI assistant. Clicking it will usually open a Bolt chat in a separate panel or tab, allowing you to ask coding questions or get AI help while you're working in StackBlitz. Essentially, you can pull up your AI assistant on demand—it may open Bolt in a new browser tab with your project context loaded.

The interface is designed to keep everything you need in view: your code and the running result side by side, with tools and logs easily accessible. Spend a moment exploring these areas—click on files, examine the preview, and familiarize yourself with where everything is located in your project.

Editing Your Code with Immediate Feedback

One of the best parts of using StackBlitz is the live development experience, which creates an incredibly tight feedback loop between writing code and seeing results. Let's try making a simple change to see this in action. Open one of your project's source files, such as the main component or main page of your app (for example, a file where the list of movies is rendered). Now make a small edit. For instance, if there is a title text in your app's header that says "Movie Explorer," try changing that string in the code to say "My Amazing Movie App" instead.

As soon as you stop typing for a moment, StackBlitz will automatically recompile and refresh the preview. You should see the app preview update the title to "My Amazing Movie App" almost immediately. This is *hot reloading* in action—StackBlitz detects your file change and updates the running app without requiring a manual refresh.

You can use this rapid feedback loop to experiment and learn. For example, if you're curious how changing a number affects a layout, what happens if you modify an API endpoint, or how different styling approaches look, you can change the code and watch the result instantly. This encourages tinkering, which is a great way to understand the codebase that Bolt generated for you.

Here are several additional features you might find useful while developing in StackBlitz's editor:

Autosave

By default, StackBlitz autosaves your changes and triggers a live reload. You might notice that as you pause typing, a small "Saving..." indicator appears or the Save button becomes active. You can also manually save (for example, by pressing Ctrl+S or Cmd+S) if needed. If for some reason you want to turn off autosave (say you want to make a batch of changes before the app reloads), you can find that setting in the Settings menu. But generally, autosave combined with hot reload is very convenient.

Undo/Redo

The editor supports the usual undo (Ctrl+Z or Cmd+Z) and redo (Ctrl+Y or Cmd+Shift+Z) operations. Don't hesitate to undo a change if something breaks, and then try again.

Find in files

Need to find where a certain word or function is used? Use the search icon (often on the left sidebar) or press Ctrl+Shift+F (Cmd+Shift+F on Mac) to search across all files in your project. This is helpful if you want to quickly locate where, say, the "TMDB API key" is referenced or which file contains the function `fetch Movies()`.

File operations

You can create new files or folders via the file explorer. Look for a + icon or right-click in the explorer area. For instance, if you want to add a new component or script file for a feature, you can do it here. You can also rename or delete files (right-click or use the context menu on a file). All these changes take effect immediately in the environment.

Preview in a new window

If the embedded preview is too small or you want to see the app in a full tab, click the "Open in New Window" button (often an icon of an external arrow or window). This will open your running app in a separate browser tab. The URL will be something like *https://<project-id>.webcontainer.io* or a similar StackBlitz-generated URL. You can interact with your app there as a normal web page. This is also handy if you want to share the running app with someone; they can visit that URL (as long as your project is public or you've shared it) and see the app in action.

Debugging and Testing in StackBlitz

As you develop, you'll inevitably run into bugs or want to test new functionality. StackBlitz provides several tools to help with this process:

Console logs and error handling
> If you want to debug something, use `console.log()` in your code. The message will appear in the console panel at the bottom. If an error happens, check the console panel for red error messages—clicking an error might even highlight the corresponding file and line in the editor. This immediate access to console output eliminates the need to constantly switch to browser developer tools for basic debugging.

Browser DevTools integration
> The preview pane is basically a browser view, so you can right-click inside the preview and choose "Inspect" to open the browser's Developer Tools for that preview. This lets you inspect the HTML/CSS, see console output (in the browser console), and monitor network requests. It's the same as opening DevTools on any web page—extremely useful for debugging styling issues or monitoring API calls to services like TMDB.

Unit testing capabilities
> If Bolt generated any tests with your project (it does with some frameworks), you can run them as well. This might require opening a terminal and running a command like `npm test`. StackBlitz's WebContainers can run those tests in the browser environment, giving you immediate feedback on code quality and functionality.

Project history and snapshots
> StackBlitz doesn't have full version control by default unless you connect it to GitHub, but it does save your project state. If you accidentally mess something up, there's an option to revert to previous save points, or you can use the editor's Undo button. In some cases, if you refresh the whole page, it will load the last saved state of your project. As a best practice, save your work often and consider GitHub integration for true version control.

By now, you should feel more comfortable navigating and using the StackBlitz editor. You've opened files, made edits, and seen your app respond instantly. This hands-on development is where you'll spend most of your time in StackBlitz. Next, we'll discuss how this workflow differs from what you experienced in Bolt, so you can adjust your mindset and make the most of both tools.

Workflow Differences Between Bolt and StackBlitz

As a developer who started with Bolt, you experienced a very different workflow compared to traditional coding. Let's explore the key differences between the AI-driven Bolt workflow and the manual StackBlitz workflow. Understanding these differences will help you transition smoothly and leverage the strengths of each approach.

From AI Prompts to Direct Coding

In Bolt, you begin by describing what you want in plain English. The AI interprets your request and generates code for you. The primary mode of "writing code" is through writing natural-language prompts and letting the AI produce the result. Its primary mode of interaction is natural-language prompts and AI suggestions.

StackBlitz shifts you to a more traditional, hands-on coding approach: you open the code that Bolt created and edit it directly. You have full control now. If you need a new feature or change, instead of requesting the AI to "please add X," you will implement it by writing or modifying the code yourself. For example, if you want to add a search bar feature in StackBlitz, you'd manually write the HTML for an input field and the JavaScript/TypeScript logic to handle search queries. You're writing the instructions in code, not in English. The feedback loop is immediate (as you saw with live preview), but the creative effort is yours. This might feel slower than Bolt's instant AI generation, but it gives you complete precision over the outcome. It's how you gain a deeper understanding of your app's workings—and it's an essential skill as you progress in development.

Editing and Refinement

In Bolt, if you wanted to tweak something, you likely issued another prompt or command to the AI to adjust it. Sometimes the AI got it right, sometimes not, and you might have had to rephrase or refine your prompt to get the desired result.

In StackBlitz, *you* are the one finding and fixing issues and making tweaks. This means reading the code to locate the thing you want to change (maybe a CSS style or a function's logic) and then editing it. The advantage is that you can make the change exactly as you envision, with no ambiguity. There's no need to guess how to phrase a request so the AI does it—you just do it. This requires a bit more knowledge from you; you'll need to identify which part of the code is responsible for the behavior you want to change. This is where using tools like search or DevTools to inspect elements or console logs can help you pinpoint the right spot. It's perfectly fine if at first you have to do some trial and error: for example, change a value, see what happens, and iterate until it looks right.

Over time, you'll build a mental map of the codebase. You'll remember, "Oh, the movie card layout is defined in `MovieCard.css`—I can tweak its styles there," or "The API call is made in `moviesService.js`—that's where the fetch URL and API key are set."

It's normal to feel a learning curve here. Going from "the AI does what I describe" to "I do it myself in code" is a transition. But as you practice, you'll likely find your confidence growing. Many developers find this process rewarding because you gain a clearer understanding of how everything fits together. And remember, if you get stuck, you can still use resources like Bolt's "Ask" feature or search online for solutions—StackBlitz just puts you in the driver's seat for implementing them.

Project Structure and Visibility

Another key difference is how much of the project's inner workings you see. Bolt tries to keep things abstracted. It doesn't show you every file unless you ask, and it handles setup tasks (like creating a *package.json*, installing libraries, configuring build tools) behind the scenes. It's a bit of a black box that delivers a working result.

StackBlitz, in contrast, lays everything out on the table. When you open the project in StackBlitz, you see all the files Bolt created: the source code, configuration files, dependency lists, and so on. This transparency might reveal things you didn't need to think about in Bolt, such as:

- Your app's dependencies (the libraries it uses) are listed in *package.json*. For example, you might discover your project uses a library like Axios for HTTP requests or a UI framework, which Bolt included automatically. Now you can see those listed explicitly.

- Build or configuration files (depending on your framework): for instance, if it's a React project, you might see a *vite.config.js*; if Angular, maybe some environment config. These files define how the project is built and served.

- Environment or config files, such as a place where an API key or base URL might be stored. Bolt might have injected your TMDB API key somewhere in the code or a config; now, in StackBlitz, you can find exactly where that is.

Don't be intimidated by these files. You don't necessarily need to modify them immediately, but it's good to know they exist. As you progress, you might peek into them to understand how things are wired up. StackBlitz essentially demystifies what Bolt sets up for you automatically. For instance, if you're curious how the development server is started, look at the *package.json* "scripts" section—there's likely a script like "start": "react-scripts start" or similar that Bolt ran behind the scenes. If you wonder where the app gets the base URL for the TMDB API, you might find it defined as a constant in a file or in an environment variable. Seeing the full structure helps you become a more self-sufficient developer, because you know what each piece of the project is for.

AI Assistance in StackBlitz

Do you lose all AI help when you move to StackBlitz? Not entirely. StackBlitz is primarily about manual editing, but it doesn't leave you without support. As noted, there's the "Ask Bolt" button that can bring up Bolt's AI assistant. Additionally, StackBlitz allows you to use GitHub's Copilot (an AI code-completion tool) if you have access to that, or other AI extensions. The difference is that in StackBlitz, the AI takes a backseat unless you explicitly call on it. It won't rewrite large chunks of your app spontaneously (unless you copy-paste code from somewhere); instead, it might autocomplete a line or suggest how to fix a small error.

If you ever feel stuck writing a piece of code in StackBlitz, you can certainly ask the AI for help. For example, you might open the Bolt chat and ask, "How do I filter the movie list by title?" and it could give you guidance or even a code snippet. You would then integrate that snippet manually into your project. This hybrid approach can be powerful: you're learning to code and leaning on AI as a tutor or helper when needed rather than letting it do everything. Now Bolt functions more like an on-demand mentor you can consult, while you remain in control of the editor.

Saving and Versioning

In Bolt, your project is saved in the cloud (tied to your account or session), but there isn't a concept of version control exposed to you. If you made a mistake, you might have asked Bolt to fix it or, at worst, restarted the project. There was no explicit history of each change you made, aside from the chat history.

In StackBlitz, you have more agency to save and manage versions of your project. The Save button will save the current state of the project to your StackBlitz account. If you're logged in, each save is recorded, and StackBlitz even keeps some history of your edits (you might see a basic timeline or have the ability to "rewind" to a previous save point via the project's menu). This isn't a full version control system by itself, but it's a step in that direction.

More importantly, StackBlitz allows you to integrate with GitHub for true version control (which we'll cover shortly). With GitHub, you can have commits, branches, and pull requests just like any professional project. But even before using Git, it's good to develop a habit of making logical, incremental changes and saving your work. If you're about to attempt a big change, you might hit "Fork" in StackBlitz to create a separate copy of the project (so you can experiment without messing up the original). Or after a major feature is completed and working, consider exporting to GitHub or downloading a backup.

In essence, StackBlitz moves you into a more professional development workflow, where you think about your changes, test them, and save them systematically. It's less ad hoc than relying on AI to regenerate parts of your app on the fly. This structure might feel more rigid, but it sets you up with good habits that will scale well when you're working on larger projects or in teams.

Table 10-1 summarizes the key differences between working in Bolt and working in StackBlitz.

Table 10-1. Key differences between the Bolt and StackBlitz development workflows

Aspect	Bolt workflow	StackBlitz workflow
Initiating changes	You describe changes in natural language to AI.	You implement changes by writing/editing code directly.
Speed vs. control	Very fast initial results: AI writes the code in seconds.	Slower to implement (you write code), but you have complete control over the outcome.
Learning curve	Easy to start; you don't need to know syntax for the initial app.	You engage with actual code, which may require learning programming languages and/or framework details, vastly improving your skills.
Error handling	You prompt the AI to fix errors.	You read error messages and debug them yourself (with the aid of tools and possibly AI suggestions).
Project insight	Abstracted; you see high-level results.	Transparent; you see all files and inner workings.
Saving progress	Project saved in Bolt cloud (limited version history through chat context)	Project saved in StackBlitz (explicit saves). Option to use full version control with GitHub integration.

By recognizing these differences, you can mentally prepare for the shift. Many developers use Bolt to kickstart a project, then use StackBlitz (and eventually local development or other tools) to carry it forward. You're following a path that many will likely adopt: *AI-assisted beginning, human-driven continuation.* You get the best of both worlds: speed and convenience upfront, and unlimited control and learning as you move forward.

Using the Integrated Terminal

While the StackBlitz UI provides a lot of point-and-click convenience, sometimes you need the power of a good old terminal. The terminal in StackBlitz is like the command-line interface on your computer, except it's running inside that WebContainer environment in your browser. Let's look at how to use it and what you might need it for.

To open a terminal in StackBlitz, look for a terminal icon or prompt symbol (often >_) in the interface. In the classic StackBlitz editor, there may be a dedicated Terminal button or an entry under a menu (e.g., Terminal → New Terminal). In the newer StackBlitz environment, you might open the bottom panel and then click + to start a new terminal tab. If your project is already running a process (like a dev server),

StackBlitz might have automatically opened a terminal tab to show that process's output. For instance, when you exported your project, if it started with npm start or ng serve, you likely saw a terminal panel with logs of that server starting up.

In any case, once you have the terminal open, you can type commands just like you would on a local machine. The StackBlitz WebContainer runs a Linux-like environment. Here are some useful commands and scenarios:

Basic navigation
You can type ls to list files in the current directory or pwd to print the working directory. By default, the terminal starts in your project's root folder (where your project files are). You can use cd foldername to navigate into a folder.

Installing packages
One common use of the terminal is to add new dependencies. For example, if you want to install a library like Lodash or Chart.js, you can run npm install lodash or npm install chart.js. StackBlitz will fetch the package and update your *package.json* accordingly. Once the install finishes, you can immediately import that package in your code. No need to refresh or do anything else—the environment is updated on the fly. (Behind the scenes, StackBlitz's WebContainer is doing something similar to running npm install on your machine, but it's confined to the browser.)

Running scripts or tools
Check your project's *package.json* for a "scripts" section. Often, you'll see scripts like build, test, or lint. You can run these with npm run build or npm test, etc., in the terminal. For example, if Bolt set up some unit tests for your app, you could execute npm test and see the tests run in the terminal output. Or you might run a build to prepare a production version of your app by running npm run build. The ability to run such commands means you're not limited by the StackBlitz UI; you have the full power of Node's tooling available.

Starting additional servers or processes
Suppose you add a new server file or some background script. You can run it in the terminal. For instance, if you created an Express server file (server.js), you could launch it by typing node server.js. The server would start inside the WebContainer, and if it listens on a port, StackBlitz will even make that available (often via a URL like *https://<project-id>.webcontainer.io* with a port or path). StackBlitz might show an indicator (in the Ports sidebar) for any server processes that open a port.

There are a few things to keep in mind with the terminal and WebContainers. First, the WebContainer is ephemeral. If you close the StackBlitz tab or refresh it, any running processes in the terminal will stop. When you reopen the project, it will set up the environment fresh and usually autorun the start script again. So if you manually started something (say a custom server), you'll need to run that command again if you refresh or reopen the project.

You can open multiple terminal tabs if needed. For example, you might have one terminal running `npm start` to keep the dev server up, and open a second terminal to run other commands like testing or installing packages. Look for a + or New Terminal option to get another terminal instance.

The terminal environment has some limitations. It's pretty complete for Node.js work, but not everything is identical to a full Linux VM. For example, certain system-level operations or installing system packages won't work (you don't have sudo, and you can't apt-get install things in a sandbox). Also, at the time of writing, StackBlitz's WebContainer doesn't include a Git client in the terminal by default (for security reasons). That means you won't use Git commands inside the StackBlitz terminal. Instead, you'll use StackBlitz's interface to connect to GitHub (or do Git operations on your local machine if you download the project). I'll cover the GitHub integration in the next section.

To illustrate a typical terminal use case, imagine you want to add a chart to your movie app to visualize some data (perhaps the number of movies by genre). You find a package called chart.js that can do this. In StackBlitz's terminal, you run `npm install chart.js`. After a short moment, the package is installed. You see it added to *package.json* under dependencies. Now you can write in your code import `{ Chart }` from `'chart.js'`; and proceed to use it to render a chart. If the package had any issues or needed polyfills, the terminal would show errors, and you could troubleshoot from there (maybe by reading the documentation or searching online). But in most cases, straightforward packages will just work.

Using the integrated terminal can make you feel like StackBlitz is truly "your machine in the cloud." It's an excellent way to get comfortable with command-line tools in a safe environment. If you're new to using the terminal, this is a gentle introduction: you can't break your real system, and if something goes wrong, you can just refresh the page to reset the environment.

GitHub Integration for Version Control and Collaboration

Sooner or later, as your project grows or you want to collaborate with others, you'll want to put your code on GitHub (or another Git repository platform). StackBlitz provides integration to make this easy, effectively bridging the gap between the in-browser environment and external repositories. Connecting to GitHub gives you full version control with commits, branches, and pull requests—essential for professional development. It also serves as a backup of your code outside StackBlitz, and opens up possibilities like deploying your site via GitHub Pages or other CI/CD workflows.

There are two common ways to get your StackBlitz project on GitHub. Create a new GitHub repo from StackBlitz and push your code to it, or import an existing GitHub repo into StackBlitz. For our scenario (starting from a Bolt project that's now in StackBlitz), we'll focus on the first: creating a new repo and pushing the code there. Here's how to do it:

1. *Connect to GitHub through StackBlitz.*

   In the StackBlitz editor, find the option to connect a repository. If you're using the classic StackBlitz editor interface, there will be a Connect Repository button in the Project sidebar (usually at the top of the file explorer panel). It might have a GitHub icon or say, "Connect to GitHub." Click that. If it's your first time using this feature, StackBlitz will prompt you to authorize your GitHub account. Follow the steps to log in to GitHub and authorize StackBlitz (you might see a pop-up window for this). Once authorized, the Connect Repository dialog will appear.

2. *Create a new repository from your project.*

   In the dialog, you should see an option to create a new repository (as opposed to importing into an existing repo). Select the option to create a new GitHub repository. You'll be asked to enter a repository name. For example, you might name it "movie-explorer-app" or something descriptive. After entering a name, click the button to Create repository and push (the wording might be "Create repo & push" or similar). StackBlitz will then take care of setting up a new repository in your GitHub account and pushing all the current project files to that repo. This usually happens quickly, and you'll get a confirmation that the project is now connected to GitHub.

3. *Verify the repository.*

   You can go to GitHub (*https://github.com*) and check your account's repositories—you should see the new repo with your project name, containing all the files of your StackBlitz project. At this point, your code is safely stored on GitHub as well as in StackBlitz. By default, StackBlitz creates the repo as private (if you're on a free GitHub plan, private repos are allowed). You can make it public in GitHub settings if you want others to see it. The branch will be main (or master in some cases), and that's where your code resides.

4. *Continue development and commit changes.*

   After connecting to GitHub, StackBlitz's interface will typically show a Commit button (often in the top toolbar, near the Save button). When you make further changes in StackBlitz, you can click Commit to push those changes to GitHub. It may prompt you to enter a commit message describing the changes. For example, if you added a search feature, you might write a commit message like "Add search bar to filter movies." Each commit will update the GitHub repository.

This means your StackBlitz project and the GitHub repo stay in sync. If you forget to commit, don't worry—your changes are still live in StackBlitz, but they just won't be on GitHub until you commit them. It's good practice to commit relatively often, especially after completing a feature or a fix, so that your GitHub repository reflects the latest working state of your app.

Once your project is on GitHub, you and others can use the full spectrum of GitHub features. If you want someone else to contribute, they can fork the repo or you can add them as a collaborator. They could even open the repository directly in StackBlitz on their end (StackBlitz allows opening a GitHub repo by URL) and play with it or propose changes.

You might want to use branches to work on big changes without affecting the main line. While StackBlitz's UI for branch management is limited (it primarily works with the main branch through the UI), you *can* create new branches by going to GitHub and doing it there, or using Bolt's GitHub integration (Bolt's interface actually supports branching, as we'll mention). For a beginner, it's perfectly fine to stick to the main branch initially. If you do use branches, you might handle the branching and merging on GitHub's website or via a local clone.

With your code on GitHub, you can use services like Netlify, Vercel, or GitHub Pages to deploy your app. Some of these can be set up to automatically deploy whenever you push a new commit to a specific branch (continuous deployment). This is beyond our scope here, but know that getting your code on GitHub is the first step to many other developer workflows.

After exporting to GitHub, you might wonder: can you go back to using Bolt's AI on this project? The answer is yes—going from Bolt to GitHub isn't a one-way journey. In fact, Bolt has an "Import from GitHub" feature. You could go to the Bolt.new home page and choose to import an existing repository (it will ask you to log in to GitHub and select a repo). If you import the repo you just pushed, Bolt will load that project and you'll be able to chat with the AI about the code, have it make suggestions, or even let it generate further changes. Bolt's AI will only see the code on the branch you import (usually the main branch), and it can then assist you with that context. This means you have a flexible workflow: you can bounce between AI-assisted development and manual coding as needed. Perhaps you'll code manually in StackBlitz for a while, then hit a snag and decide to ask Bolt for help on a tricky function. Just import the latest code to Bolt and get AI advice, and you could even have Bolt implement something on a new branch then merge it back via GitHub. The possibilities are wide.

Summary

To keep things simple, let's recap what we've achieved in this chapter: you took an app that was initially built with AI assistance, moved it into a full coding environment without needing to install anything locally, and continued development with full control. Along the way, you learned how StackBlitz's in-browser IDE works, how WebContainers allow running server code in the browser, how to navigate and edit your project's code, and how to integrate with GitHub for version control. You've bridged the gap between a no-code (or low-code) beginning and a coding-centric workflow. This combination of AI tools and cloud development is a powerful approach for modern web development.

In the next chapter, you'll see how Bolt's integration with Expo allows us to build native mobile apps and convert web apps into mobile.

CHAPTER 11

Building Native Mobile Apps Using Bolt and Expo

Bolt.new supports native mobile apps through a partnership with Expo, a framework and tooling for developing React Native apps. This integration allows developers to build iOS and Android applications entirely in the browser by simply describing the app, merging the power of React Native with Bolt's AI-driven development.

The Expo framework provides a set of libraries for accessing native device features like cameras and sensors and a development app, Expo Go, for live previews on actual devices. Bolt integrates with Expo by running the Expo development environment inside StackBlitz's WebContainers (discussed in Chapter 10), meaning you can create, run, and preview React Native apps directly in your browser.

In this chapter, we will explore how to leverage Bolt's Expo integration to create a mobile app from scratch. We'll walk through building a location-based weather app and along the way cover mobile-specific features like accessing device location, camera, and notifications; styling with React Native; and testing on devices. Then we'll try converting your existing Grocery List web app to mobile. As with the other integrations you've seen, Bolt handles setting up the project, installing native modules, and even packaging the app for deployment based on your prompts. Bolt's web IDE lets you inspect logs and errors, and you can use React Native's debugging techniques (like logging to the console) directly within Bolt.

Setup

You'll need a smartphone with the Expo Go app installed. It's available on iOS App Store and Google Play.

Logging in to an Expo account on your device is helpful, but not strictly required, for development. You don't need Xcode or Android Studio to *develop* with Expo and Bolt, but if you eventually want to publish your app, you will need an Apple Developer account (for iOS) and/or a Google Play Developer account (for Android). For now, we'll focus on development and testing.

To start a Bolt + Expo project, you can either select the Expo starter template on the Bolt home page or simply prompt Bolt. It will initialize a React Native project with Expo under the hood and then proceed to implement features as you describe them. Once the project is initialized, you'll typically see a file called *App.js* or *App.tsx*, and some initial code running a default app. From here, you can start guiding Bolt to build the features you want.

Let's build a practical example: a weather app we'll call LocalWeather that shows the current weather at the user's location. This example will demonstrate how to build an app using Bolt prompts that uses one device capability (geolocation) and calls an external API (a weather service).

Initial Prompt and Location Services

Start by telling Bolt what you want to build:

> Create a new Expo React Native app called "LocalWeather." It should ask for the user's location and then display the current weather for that location.

When you provide this prompt, Bolt will:

- Initialize a new Expo app, generating files including *package.json* and *App.tsx*.
- Install the necessary Expo packages; in this case, for location services, Bolt should install the *expo-location* package, which is part of Expo's software development kit (SDK).
- Write code in *App.tsx* to request the user's permission to use their location and then fetch their current GPS coordinates.
- Set up a basic UI to display weather information (since we haven't told it which weather API to use, it could either leave a placeholder or ask for clarification).

After processing the prompt, Bolt will produce a draft *App.tsx* file that looks something like this simplified example:

```
import React, { useEffect, useState } from 'react';

import { Text, View } from 'react-native';

import * as Location from 'expo-location';

export default function App() {
```

```
  const [location, setLocation] = useState(null);

  const [errorMsg, setErrorMsg] = useState(null);

  useEffect(() => {

    (async () => {

      let { status } = await Location.requestForegroundPermissionsAsync();

      if (status !== 'granted') {

        setErrorMsg('Permission to access location was denied');

        return;

      }

      let loc = await Location.getCurrentPositionAsync({});

      setLocation(loc.coords);

    })();

  }, []);

  return (

    <View style={{ flex: 1, alignItems: 'center', justifyContent: 'center' }}>

      {location ? (

        <Text>Latitude: {location.latitude}, Longitude: {location.longitude}
        </Text>

      ) : (

        <Text>{errorMsg || "Fetching location..."}</Text>

      )}

    </View>

  );

}
```

Even if your code isn't exactly like this, Bolt should handle the core idea: requesting permission and getting the user's current latitude/longitude.

You can already test this on your device via Expo Go. When you scan the QR code and open the app, you should see it asking for location permission. On a device, Expo will automatically handle showing the permission dialog. Once you grant permission, it will display the coordinates. This confirms that Bolt has successfully integrated Expo's Location API.

Now that we have the device location, the next step is determining the weather for that location.

Integrating a Weather API

To get actual weather data, we'll use an external weather API. A popular choice is the OpenWeatherMap API (*https://openweathermap.org/api*), which provides current weather and forecast data. OpenWeatherMap requires an API key (a free tier (*https:// openweathermap.org/price*) is available). You'll need to register on the site to get a key, which can take a few minutes to activate.

Note: we're only fetching the *current* weather here (that is, the temperature and conditions right now). If you want to display *forecasts* (hourly or multiday), OpenWeatherMap and similar APIs offer those, too, but you'll need to use their separate forecast endpoints and parse that data accordingly.

Once you have obtained an API key, prompt Bolt to use OpenWeatherMap to fetch weather info:

> Use the OpenWeatherMap API to get the current weather for the user's location. The API key is stored in an environment variable `OWM_API_KEY`. Display the city name, temperature, and a description of the weather (e.g., "Sunny").

Here's what we're conveying:

- That we have an API key in an environment variable, so we expect Bolt not to hardcode it. If the project doesn't have one yet, Bolt will likely instruct us to add it to an *.env* file or a secure storage. Bolt may open a secure prompt for the API key or ask us to add it via the UI.

- Which API to call and what data to retrieve (e.g., city name, temperature, description).

- How to present it.

Bolt will then generate code to call OpenWeatherMap's Current Weather API. Typically, that involves constructing a URL like this: *http://api.openweathermap.org/ data/2.5/weather?lat={lat}&lon={lon}&appid={API_KEY}&units=metric* (including `units=metric` for Celsius or `units=imperial` for Fahrenheit).

Bolt will use `fetch` or Axios to call this endpoint. In React Native (especially in Expo), using `fetch` is straightforward. The response will be JSON, containing fields like `name` (city), `main.temp` (temperature), and `weather[0].description` (description). Bolt knows, or can infer, what to extract. It should also handle the asynchronous nature of the call with either `async/await` or `.then()`.

After this prompt, Bolt will update *App.tsx* or create a new component for Weather. Let's assume it extends *App.tsx*. Here's some pseudo code to give you a feel for it:

```
const [weather, setWeather] = useState(null);

useEffect(() => {

  (async () => {

    ... // after getting location as loc.coords

    if (loc?.coords) {

      try {

        const response = await fetch(
          `https://api.openweathermap.org/data/2.5/weather?lat=${loc.
            coords.latitude}&lon=${loc.coords.longitude}&
            units=metric&appid=${process.env.OWM_API_KEY}`);

        const data = await response.json();

        setWeather({

          city: data.name,

          temp: Math.round(data.main.temp),

          description: data.weather[0].description

        });

      } catch (err) {

        console.error(err);

      }

    }

  })();

}, [location]);
```

Here's what Bolt typically generates for the JavaScript part of the weather UI, to render weather information:

```
<View style={styles.container}>
  {weather ? (
    <View>
      <Text style={styles.city}>{weather.city}</Text>
      <Text style={styles.temp}>{weather.temp}°C</Text>
      <Text style={styles.desc}>{weather.description}</Text>
    </View>
  ) : (
    <Text>{errorMsg || "Loading weather..."}</Text>
  )}
</View>
```

Here's what Bolt will do with this code:

- Create a new state, `weather`, to hold the fetched data
- Construct the API URL with our latitude/longitude and insert the `OWM_API_KEY` from environment
- Parse the JSON and pick the needed fields
- Update the UI to display the weather info nicely (including a °C symbol and some styling)
- Possibly add some basic styles in a `StyleSheet.create` (for `styles.container`, `styles.city`, etc.)

To test this, run the app again in Expo Go. You should now see the city name and temperature on your device's screen, as shown in Figure 11-1.

Bolt might default to lowercase; you can always prompt it with refinements:

> Capitalize the weather description.

If something isn't quite right—like if you see "Loading weather..." indefinitely—that means either the API call failed or the state didn't update. You can open the console logs in the Bolt editor to check for errors.

At this stage, we have a functional weather app that gets user location and fetches data. Let's enhance it further by incorporating more mobile-specific features to illustrate Bolt's capabilities.

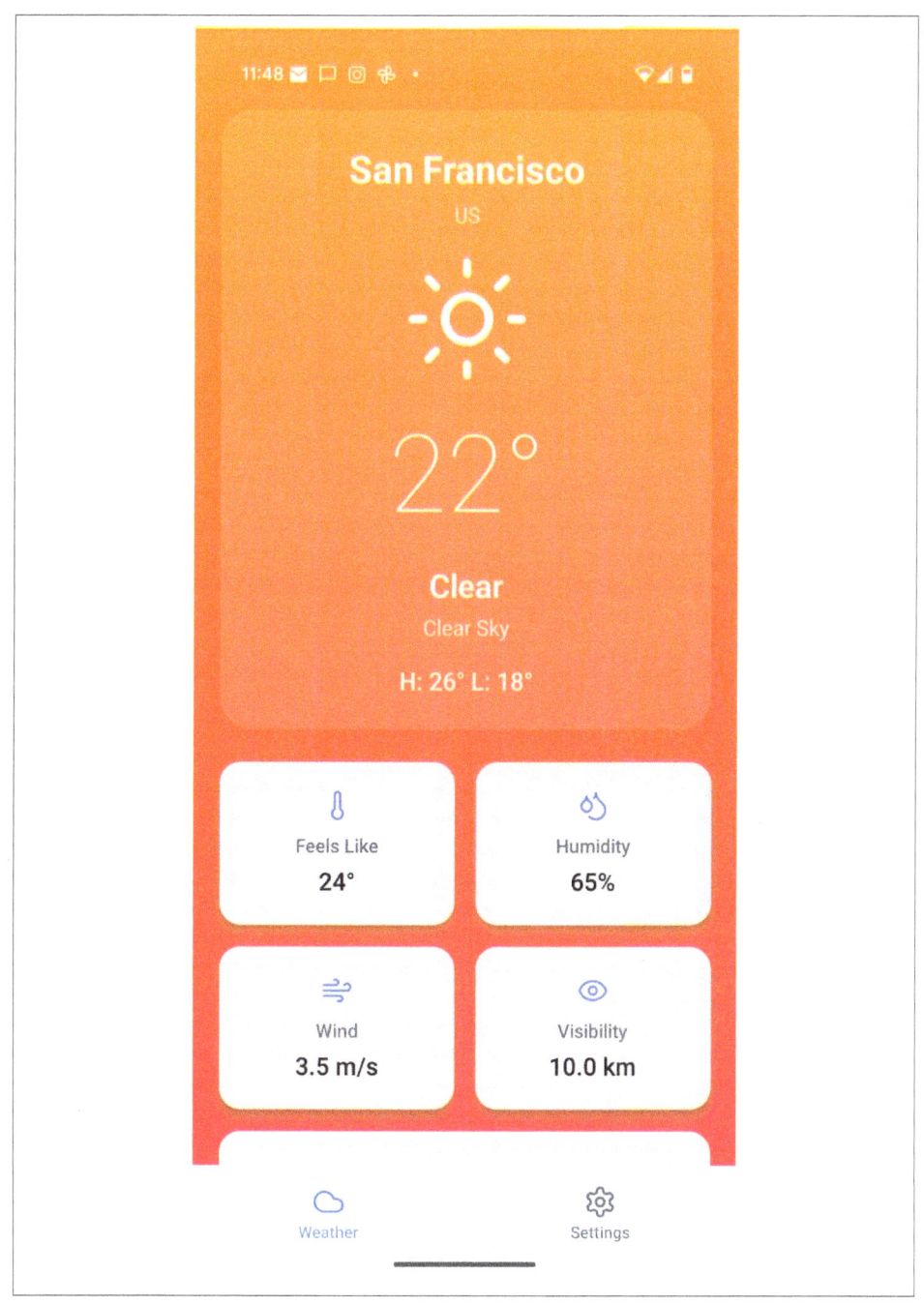

Figure 11-1. The weather app showing city name and current weather

Using Device Features: Camera and Notifications

Our weather app is simple, but we can extend it with some mobile-native features. We'll cover two here:

- A button to take a photo—perhaps of the sky, to compare with the reported weather—just for fun
- Optional daily weather forecast notifications, scheduled at a certain time

These features involve using Expo's Camera and Notifications APIs.

Accessing the Camera

Expo provides an `expo-camera` API for camera access. We can prompt Bolt to use this to add a camera feature:

> Add a feature to take a photo of the current weather view. When the user taps a "Take Photo" button, open the camera, allow them to capture an image, and then return to the app, showing a thumbnail of the photo.

Here's what you should expect Bolt to do:

- Install `expo-camera` (if it hasn't already)
- Request camera permissions
- Add a UI element (a button) to launch the camera
- Possibly create a separate component or screen for the camera preview, using Expo's API
- Add code to capture the photo, return the image URI, and display the photo, possibly with an `Image` component to show the thumbnail

Bolt might create a new component with a name like `CameraView` or handle it in *App.tsx* with a conditional view. It could navigate, if it sets up a basic navigation stack, or simply toggle a state to show the camera preview, something like this:

```
import { Button, Image } from 'react-native';

import { Camera } from 'expo-camera';

const [hasCamPerm, setHasCamPerm] = useState<boolean|null>(null);

const [cameraRef, setCameraRef] = useState<Camera|null>(null);

const [photo, setPhoto] = useState(null);

useEffect(() => {
```

```
(async () => {

  const { status } = await Camera.requestCameraPermissionsAsync();

  setHasCamPerm(status === 'granted');

})();

}, []);

async function takePhoto() {

  if(cameraRef){

    const photoData = await cameraRef.takePictureAsync();

    setPhoto(photoData.uri);

  }

}

...

{ hasCamPerm ? (

    <>

      {photo ? <Image source={{ uri: photo }}
              style={{ width: 100, height: 100 }} /> : null}

      <Camera style={{ width: 300, height: 400 }}
       ref={ref => setCameraRef(ref)} />

      <Button title="Snap Photo" onPress={takePhoto} />

    </>

  ) : (

    <Text>Camera permission not granted</Text>

  )

}
```

This is a rough idea. Since, as you know, Bolt is nondeterministic, it might actually handle it differently: for example, it might open the camera in a full-screen view and then return. The key is that with the prompt, Bolt will wire up the permission and camera-usage logic. The user can then take a picture and see a thumbnail. If you want to play with enhancing the app later on, you could prompt Bolt to upload that photo to a server.

Scheduling Notifications

Expo's notifications API (expo-notifications) allows scheduling local notifications or configuring push notifications. We'll try a local daily notification:

> Add a feature to send a local notification every day at 8:00 A.M. with the current temperature and weather description.

Bolt will need to:

- Install expo-notifications.
- Request notification permissions (Notifications.requestPermissionsAsync()).
- Schedule a repeating notification.

Expo provides Notifications.scheduleNotificationAsync() with a trigger, which can be time-based. To schedule daily notifications, we can specify an interval or use cron-like scheduling.

It might produce code along these lines:

```
import * as Notifications from 'expo-notifications';

useEffect(() => {

  Notifications.requestPermissionsAsync().then(status => {

    if (status.granted) {

      Notifications.cancelAllScheduledNotificationsAsync(); // clear old if any

      Notifications.scheduleNotificationAsync({

        content: {

          title: "Today's Weather",

          body: weather

            ? `${weather.city}: ${weather.temp}°C and ${weather.description}`

            : "Check today's weather!"

        },

        trigger: {
```

```
        hour: 8,

        minute: 0,

        repeats: true
      }
    });
  }
});

}, [weather]);
```

This method tells Expo to show a notification at a specific time. The `trigger` field specifies when (in this case, 8:00 A.M. every day), and the `content` field defines what to show. It's similar to scheduling a calendar reminder but in code.

This assumes that the `weather` state is up to date; a more robust approach might fetch fresh data at that time, but Bolt might keep it simple and use whatever was last fetched. The code in the previous example uses Expo's scheduling trigger for 8:00 with `repeats: true` (meaning it repeats every day) and composes a notification message from our weather state. Bolt may also add a UI toggle to enable or disable these notifications; if not, you can prompt for that.

To test these features, run the app on your device using Expo Go. When you tap the button, the camera should open (if it's integrated in the app view) or the camera preview should become visible. Taking a photo should display it.

You won't see notifications immediately, since the next notification is scheduled for 8:00 A.M. You can test by adjusting the time to a minute or two from now and waiting or by prompting a one-time immediate notification to see if it works. You can refine the behavior with additional prompts. For example:

> Only schedule notifications if the user opts in.
>
> Add a "cancel notification" button.

Styling the React Native App

Styling in React Native (and Expo) is done via JavaScript, not CSS—typically using the `StyleSheet` API or styled components. Bolt is aware of this and will use `Style Sheet.create` to define styles, or it might use inline styles as quick solutions. By default, React Native uses flexbox for layout and supports many CSS-like properties (colors, font sizes, margins), but you can't use classes or IDs like you would in web CSS.

Bolt might have created some basic styles in the app already. We can explicitly prompt for design improvements:

Apply some styling: center the content, use a larger font for the temperature, and maybe use a nice background color or image depending on weather.

Bolt will then adjust or add a StyleSheet. For instance:

```
const styles = StyleSheet.create({
  container: {
    flex: 1,
    backgroundColor: '#87cefa', // light sky blue background
    alignItems: 'center',
    justifyContent: 'center'
  },
  city: {
    fontSize: 24,
    fontWeight: '600',
    marginBottom: 4
  },
  temp: {
    fontSize: 48,
    fontWeight: 'bold'
  },
  desc: {
    fontSize: 20,
    fontStyle: 'italic'
  }
});
```

These example styles give the app a centered layout with a sky-blue background. The city name is slightly larger, the temperature is big and bold, and the description is italicized. Bolt will apply this style to the corresponding `<Text>` elements for a more visually appealing UI.

You can continue to tweak the design by describing what you want:

> Use a background image of a sky if the weather is clear, or a rain image if rainy.

Bolt could incorporate conditional backgrounds (perhaps using `ImageBackground` component):

> Use different colors for different temperatures (blue for cold, red for hot).

Bolt can add logic to change text color based on the `weather.temp` value.

Essentially, treat Bolt as your CSS author: describe the end result, and it will try to produce the style code.

Bolt can also utilize style frameworks if you mention them. In React Native, you could ask it to use a Material Design style and it will import a UI kit. You might ask it to use Tailwind CSS in a React web project. In our case, plain styles suffice, but feel free to experiment.

React Native styling doesn't support all CSS features. Bolt will generally stick to what's available, but if you ever see a style property that doesn't work (likely something web-specific), you might need to adjust. To clean things up if needed, prompt Bolt with something like this:

> Remove any unsupported CSS from styles (since this is React Native).

Testing the App on Devices

If this is your first time using Expo, here's how it works. Bolt generates a development build and shows a QR code in the preview panel. Scanning it with Expo Go (*https://expo.dev/go*) on your phone opens a live version of the app on your device. You'll see changes as you edit or prompt Bolt (Figure 11-2).

The Expo QR code functionality allows users to preview their projects on mobile devices. After installing Expo Go for iOS or Android, scan the QR code shown to get started.

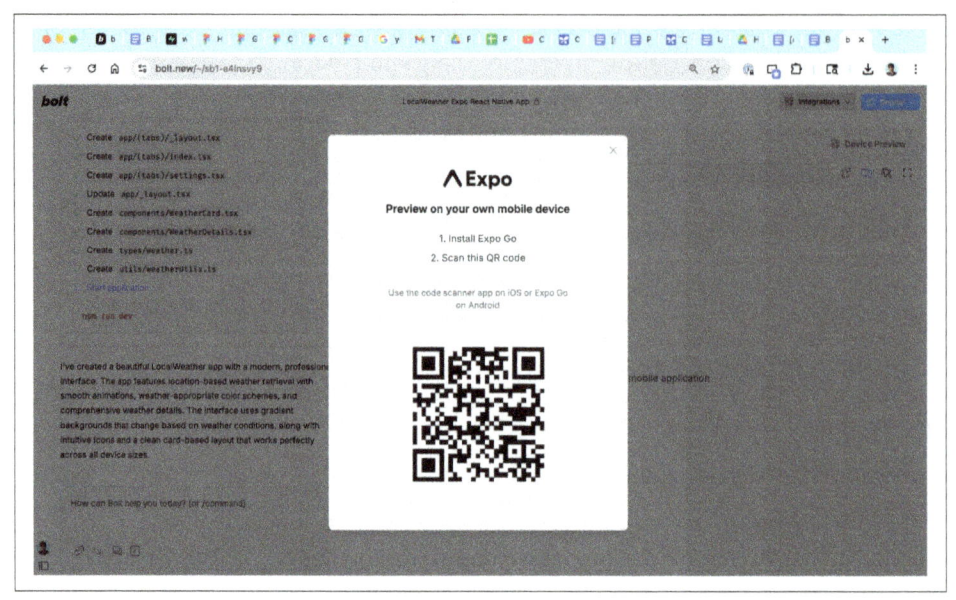

Figure 11-2. The Expo QR code functionality

Live Development Testing

Let's recap the development testing workflow. Every time you make changes via prompts or manual code edits, Bolt's web container updates and Expo's fast refresh pushes the updates to your device. You can shake the device on Android or tap the screen with two fingers on iOS to bring up the Expo dev menu. That's where you'll find features like hot reload and remote debugging. Bolt's integration is primarily about coding; for runtime debugging, you still use React Native's tools. The live preview is one of the biggest advantages: you can see your app running *as you build it*, which drastically speeds up development (Figure 11-3).

Some features, like camera and notifications, cannot be fully tested on the web preview, since they require device hardware or OS-level interactions. Using Expo Go on a physical phone is essential for those. If something doesn't work, check the device logs. You can see them in Bolt's console, or run `expo start` on your local machine and use Expo's CLI if needed. Bolt should surface any errors in its UI, however.

Bolt and Expo allow you to preview your React Native code live. The code on the left of Figure 11-3 defines a simple Home component, while on the right, you see the output on an iOS simulator/device. Any code changes will be reflected instantly on the device.

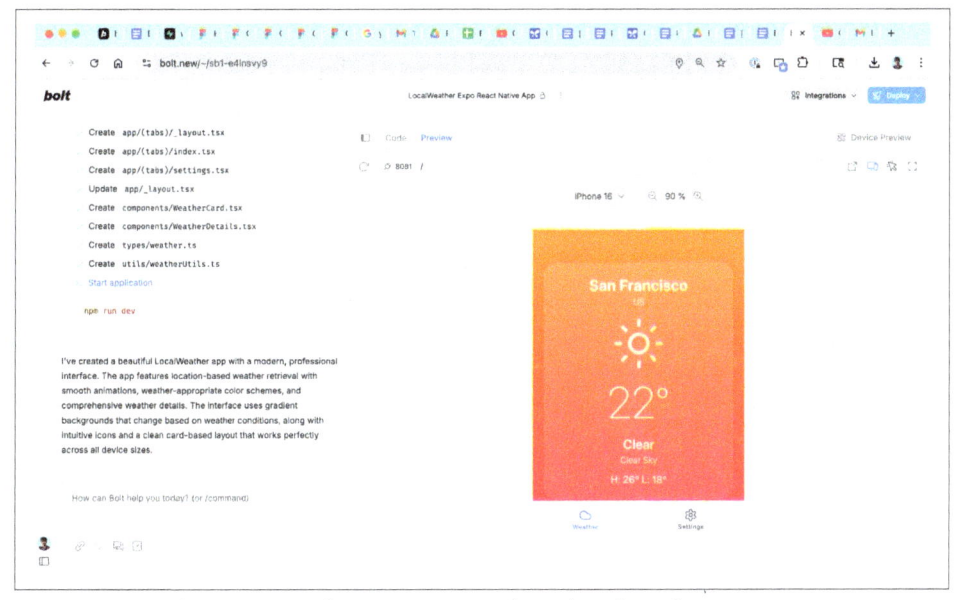

Figure 11-3. A live preview of React Native code with Bolt and Expo

Automated Testing

While our focus here is on prompt-driven development, you can also have Bolt generate automated tests for your app's logic:

> Write a Jest test for the weather-fetching function to ensure it parses API data correctly.

Bolt will create a test file that simulates an API response and checks the outcome. Be aware that writing automated tests for React Native components (with libraries like React Native Testing Library) or testing Expo modules might be advanced, but Bolt can help set it up if asked.

Production Build Testing

Expo lets you build a standalone binary (APK for Android, IPA for iOS) via Expo Application Services (EAS) (*https://expo.dev/eas*). Bolt can integrate with EAS as well for deployment. If you've deployed web apps before with StackBlitz or Netlify, think of EAS as the mobile native equivalent. Instead of pushing static assets to a CDN, you're producing signed binaries that can be submitted to the App Store or Google Play. While it's a bit more complex, EAS automates much of the process when used with Bolt.

If you prompt something like "Build the app for Android and iOS," Bolt will guide you through the process. It might not run it automatically, but it can invoke EAS CLI commands in the container. This involves having an Expo account and running `eas build`. It's beyond the scope of this chapter to fully deploy the app, but you can find detailed instructions in Expo's documentation (*https://oreil.ly/zGd20*).

Converting the Grocery List App to Mobile with Bolt

Earlier in this book (Chapter 9), you built a web-based grocery list app using Bolt. In this section, we'll walk through how to adapt that same kind of app for mobile using React Native and Expo. This is a hands-on continuation of a project you've already seen, reimagined for a different platform. Ordinarily, you'd need to rewrite a lot of code for React Native. However, Bolt can automate large parts of this conversion.

We can prompt Bolt with a description of the existing app (essentially treating it as a new project that mimics the old), or provide pieces of the existing code and ask Bolt to convert them. Bolt's AI is capable of refactoring code from one framework to another if instructed clearly.

For example, we might start a new Expo project in Bolt and say:

> I have a web app for grocery lists. It has a list of items and a form to add an item. Convert this into a React Native mobile app. Create a similar UI using React Native components. Use React Navigation for multiple screens if needed.

Bolt will interpret this and implement it:

- It will probably set up navigation, since we mentioned it. It might use the React Navigation library, since we mentioned multiple screens, or it might keep everything on one screen.
- It will replace web-specific elements with React Native ones:
  - `<div>` becomes `<View>`
  - `<span>`/`<p>` becomes `<Text>`
  - `<input>` becomes `<TextInput>`
  - `<button>` becomes `<Button>` or a `<TouchableOpacity>` with a `<Text>` label
  - CSS classes become `StyleSheet` entries—it might look at the styles if we provide them or just create new styles
- It may reuse the JavaScript logic for adding and removing items, since this can mostly remain the same: state handling with `useState` works the same way in React Native.

Bolt won't magically know about your existing web app—you have to tell it. Provide as much detail as possible. You can even copy some of your web code into the prompt; Bolt will then "read" it and transform it. This approach leverages Bolt's strength in refactoring code.

Let's say we provide some of the web code, including this snippet:

```
<div className="grocery-item">
  <input type="checkbox" checked={item.purchased}
   onChange={() => togglePurchased(item.id)} />
  <span>{item.name}</span>
  <button onClick={() => removeItem(item.id)}>Remove</button>
</div>
```

Then we ask Bolt:

Convert this component for mobile using React Native.

Bolt will output something like this:

```
<View style={styles.groceryItem}>
  <Switch value={item.purchased}
   onValueChange={() => togglePurchased(item.id)} />
  <Text style={styles.itemName}>{item.name}</Text>
  <Button title="Remove" onPress={() => removeItem(item.id)} />
</View>
```

Notice that it uses Switch, which is a React Native component for toggles. It also carries over JavaScript logic (`togglePurchased`, `removeItem`) and adjusts only the view layer. For styling, Bolt can often convert basic CSS (like margins and padding) into the React Native StyleSheet. Complex styles may need tweaking—like replacing web grid layouts with flexbox column alignment.

As always with Bolt, you'll need to use prompts iteratively to refine your app. For instance:

Make the grocery items swipeable to remove (like a swipe gesture).

Bolt could integrate a gesture handler:

Use a checkbox icon instead of Switch for purchased items.

Bolt could use the expo-vector-icons library to show a checkbox icon that toggles.

One thing to watch out for is navigation and platform differences. If your web app has multiple pages (like a settings page), Bolt might implement React Navigation with a stack or tab navigator. It will automatically add the necessary library and setup if instructed. For example:

Use React Navigation bottom tabs with the Home and Settings screens.

In response to this prompt, Bolt would add **@react-navigation/bottom-tabs** and set up a basic tab navigator.

Finally, always test the converted app thoroughly. Some things that work on the web—like1 HTML semantics or web-only libraries—have no React Native equivalent. Bolt might approximate or omit them. As you test, prompt again to refine missing features. With a few iterations, you can match your original web app's experience closely.

Summary

In this chapter, we built a native mobile app using Bolt and Expo by simply describing our intentions. We started with a weather app, tapping into device hardware (GPS and camera) and external services (a weather API and notifications). We also discussed styling and testing on real devices, and saw how Bolt can aid in porting a web app to mobile.

In the final chapter, we'll go back to Bolt to discover some advanced features and learn how to put your StackBlitz skills to use in building a backend.

CHAPTER 12

Advanced Bolt Tips

You've seen that building with Bolt is like having a tireless apprentice who can generate code almost instantly from your descriptions. But even the best apprentices make mistakes, and the most powerful tools often hide in drawers that beginners rarely open. This chapter dives deep into three advanced areas that will level up your Bolt skills: debugging techniques for when things go wrong; lesser-known productivity features that can supercharge your workflow; and backend capabilities that transform Bolt from a frontend prototyping tool into a full stack development environment.

While earlier chapters focused on the basics, this material assumes you're comfortable with fundamental web concepts (HTML, CSS, JavaScript) and ready to advance into junior developer territory. Whether you're tracking down mysterious runtime errors, preventing Bolt's AI from rewriting critical files, or building Express routes that deploy as serverless functions, the skills you'll learn here will save hours of trial and error and unlock Bolt's true potential.

Debugging

Even with AI doing the heavy lifting, things *will* go wrong—and debugging in Bolt is a skill of its own. Fortunately, Bolt provides real-time feedback as your app runs. As Bolt's website (*https://oreil.ly/voC0x*) puts it, you can see apps executed in real time and "debug errors as they occur" on the platform. Debugging a prompt-built app is a bit like being a detective solving a mystery: you gather clues (error messages, logs, and app behavior) and iteratively investigate. This section explores how to trace and fix issues in Bolt, with beginner-friendly analogies and examples.

Understanding Bolt's Live Dev Environment

Bolt runs your app in the browser using StackBlitz WebContainers (*https://oreil.ly/zB3QH*), which means it's a full Node.js environment running client and server code in-browser. (StackBlitz and WebContainers were the topic of Chapter 10.) You've seen throughout the projects in this book that when you prompt for changes, Bolt writes code and immediately runs it. If the code throws an error or fails, Bolt will detect it. For example, if a React component crashes due to a bad prop, you might see an error message in the preview or chat—Bolt's agent *notices* the exception. In one user's test (*https://oreil.ly/5FcBT*), a routing bug "[threw] an error, which [was] interestingly getting detected by Bolt." This means Bolt will typically surface runtime errors for you and display a notification or log with the stack trace, acting like a friendly alarm system.

Always read these error messages—they pinpoint *what* went wrong and *where* (for example, "TypeError in `Breadcrumb.jsx` line 42"). This is your first detective clue: the error log tells you where to look in the code. You can click the file in Bolt's editor and inspect the code around that line. Often the fix might be obvious: a variable wasn't defined or a function call is wrong. If you're not sure, ask Bolt about it (more on this in a moment).

Importantly, Bolt gives its AI agent full control over the environment, including the dev server and console, so it can restart the app or run build steps as needed. For instance, if you ask Bolt to install a library, it runs the `npm install` in the WebContainer behind the scenes. If the app needs to compile, say, a Next.js build, it will do so and show any build errors.

All these logs and errors appear right in your browser, so you don't need a separate terminal or editor. You can even open Chrome DevTools to debug. Since the backend is running inside the browser, "Node.js debugging with Chrome DevTools [...] 'just works,'" as StackBlitz's blog writes (*https://oreil.ly/eyHIU*), letting you set breakpoints or inspect objects as if it were a local app. For beginners, stepping through code in DevTools can be advanced, but it's comforting to know the option exists as you grow more confident.

Debugging and Troubleshooting in Bolt

When troubleshooting, it helps to know the usual suspects. Some common issues Bolt users encounter include:

Runtime errors
> These are code errors, and Bolt will flag them as red in the preview or logs: for example, null or undefined property access, wrong API endpoint, or a crash when a button is clicked. For instance, if clicking a generated Login button does nothing, check the browser console or Bolt's log. You might find an error like

"Uncaught ReferenceError: handleLogin is not defined." That's your cue to ask Bolt to implement or fix handleLogin. Always use the error text as a clue in your next prompt:

Fix the ReferenceError for handleLogin on login button click.

"Error loops"

Sometimes Bolt's AI will try to autofix an error and fail repeatedly. Bolt has an automatic "fix" button that appears when an error is detected (Figure 12-1). It's tempting to click it over and over, but beware: continuously "clicking the *Attempt fix* can lead to unnecessary token consumption," according to Bolt (*https://oreil.ly/wnBLB*), and the AI might loop without solving the core issue, like a doctor prescribing the same ineffective medicine repeatedly. Instead, after one attempt, step in with a new strategy.

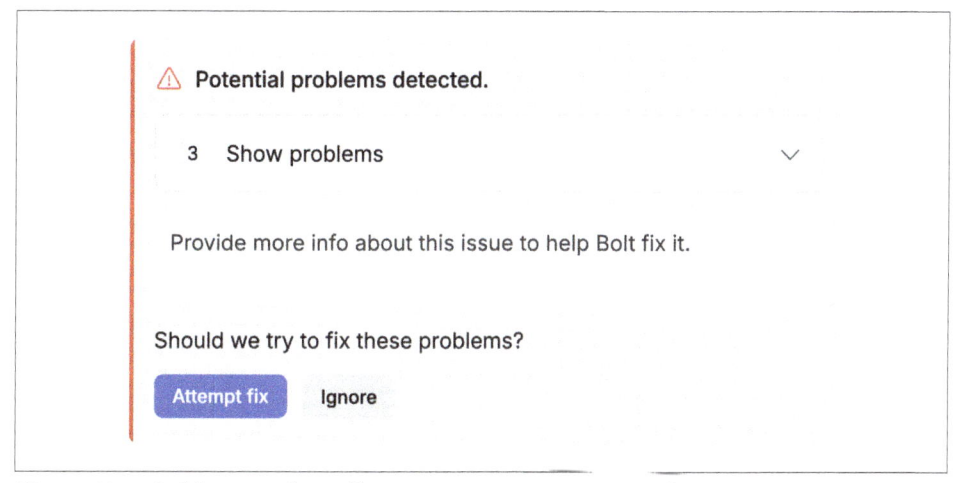

Figure 12-1. Bolt's error alert offers to attempt an automatic fix

External service errors

If your app uses external APIs (for OAuth logins, database calls, and the like), you might hit errors Bolt can't automatically solve. Examples include using lesser-known third-party libraries or APIs, where resolving errors may require additional technical research, as LLMs cannot auto-resolve all issues. For example, if Supabase returns an unauthorized error, you may need to provide a valid API key or adjust rules in Supabase, both of which are outside Bolt's immediate scope. In these cases, use Bolt's Discussion Mode or consult documentation for that service.

Environment and preview issues

Occasionally, you might see a blank preview or a generic error like "Cannot Get /" for your app. This could mean the dev server didn't start or that it built nothing at the root URL. Check that your app's start script is correct and that a home page route exists. If the WebContainer fails to start entirely (perhaps due to browser compatibility), Bolt will show a WebContainer startup error (*https://oreil.ly/SJT89*). The fix might be as simple as switching to Chrome/Edge, if you were on an unsupported browser, or disabling a blocking browser extension. If you ever get an Out of Memory (OOM) error (*https://oreil.ly/v9lPE*), that's your browser running out of RAM for the container. Closing other tabs or apps will help.

Best Practices for Debugging Bolt Apps

Debugging in Bolt is an interactive, iterative process. Here are some best practices to make it easier (and even educational):

Make one change at a time
When you have multiple issues, tackle them one by one. A good best-practice is to break big changes into smaller pieces and follow a cycle: (1) Make a change, (2) Check if the change works, (3) Move to the next feature. This is classic advice, even for human coding, but it's crucial with an AI partner. For example, if you prompt Bolt to add five new features at once and something breaks, it's harder to tell which change caused the problem. Instead, introduce features stepwise and verify each one in the app before proceeding. This way, if a bug appears, you immediately know what likely introduced it.

Read and log the code
Don't be afraid to inspect the generated code. You might notice a mistake faster than the AI. For instance, one user noticed (*https://oreil.ly/2j6lz*) that images weren't loading and, upon checking the code, realized the image URLs required an API key. Knowing that, he told Bolt to use a different image source—problem solved.

If you don't understand the code, try asking Bolt in Discussion Mode *why* it did something, or ask it to explain the code. You can also have Bolt insert logging statements. The Bolt AI is *excellent* at adding detailed logs when asked. You could prompt:

> Add `console.log` statements to show the data flow when I click "Add to Cart."

The logs will appear in the console, giving you a step-by-step trace when you test the feature.

Use Discussion Mode for help
As mentioned in Chapter 5, Bolt's Discussion Mode (*https://oreil.ly/zlP24*) lets you ask questions without modifying code. Think of it as a built-in Stack

Overflow complete with a tutor. If you hit a perplexing error or need guidance, switch to Discussion Mode and ask something like this:

Why might I be getting a 404 error when fetching */api/data*?

The AI will research and answer, possibly citing documentation or known issues. It might explain that you need to define an API route or that your backend server isn't running. Discussion Mode won't write code directly, but it often provides insight and even suggests a plan. You'll typically get an option like "Implement this fix," which, if clicked, switches back to build mode and applies the AI's proposed code changes. This separates *talking about the problem from writing code for the problem*, a beginner's lifesaver. You can clarify your understanding before making changes.

Roll your changes back if needed

If a change goes awry and you're not sure how to fix the mess, use Bolt's rollback feature to undo it. As discussed in Chapter 4, Bolt automatically creates checkpoints for each prompt in the chat history. You can scroll up to a previous message and click Rollback, which restores the project to that point in time. This is basically an undo button for your codebase—very handy if the AI's "fix" turned out worse than the original problem. Just note that rollback is permanent for anything after that checkpoint (there's no "redo"), so only use it if you're OK discarding the latest changes.

Don't overlook the obvious

Sometimes the "bug" might simply be that your prompt wasn't clear. If Bolt didn't do what you expected, consider that the instruction might have been ambiguous. Debugging a prompt can be as simple as rephrasing it or adding detail. For example, "Make the buttons blue" might not apply to a dynamically generated component unless you specify which buttons or where. In this sense, *prompt debugging* is a thing—clarifying your request is often the fix. See Chapter 3, on prompt engineering, for more.

Think of Bolt as an apprentice builder. It works fast and can put together a structure (your app) in minutes, but it might not always get everything right. Debugging is like performing a building inspection: you walk through the structure, find cracks (errors) and misalignments (features that aren't quite right), and guide the apprentice to fix them. Bolt provides you with the blueprints (the code) and warning alarms (error messages).

With practice, you'll learn to read those signals and instruct Bolt with precision to patch any issues. Every bug is an opportunity to refine your prompts or learn why the code behaved that way. By iterating methodically and using these best practices, you'll turn that initially buggy scaffold into a robust, working application.

Debugging Example

Let's walk through a simple example to tie this together. Say you prompt Bolt to create a to-do list app, and it generates a React app, where you can add and remove tasks. You excitedly test it out: the UI loads, you type a task and hit "Add"...but nothing happens. No new to-do appears on your screen. How do you debug this?

First, observe any on-screen messages or console logs. Suppose Bolt's preview shows an error banner, or you open the browser console and see "Unhandled Rejection: Failed to fetch." This tells you that the app likely tried to call a backend API and couldn't find it (thus, a 404 or failed fetch). That's a clue. Maybe Bolt set up a separate API route to save tasks, but it's not working.

In Bolt, you can open the file structure and look for any API code (perhaps a *server.js* file or an */api* folder). You find an `addTask` function in the frontend that calls `/api/addTask`, but you realize your project has no corresponding server endpoint. The AI forgot to implement the backend for it!

Now you have a clear path: you need to create a backend route. Prompt Bolt:

> The Add button is not working—create a Node/Express endpoint */api/addTask* to save new tasks (just store them in memory).

Bolt generates a backend route in the WebContainer and wires it up. Once that's done, you test again. The task adds successfully.

Now imagine that your to-dos disappear when you refresh the page. This is likely because the memory resets when the server restarts: Bolt didn't add persistence. That means your next bug (or missing feature) is a lack of storage. You could use Discussion Mode to ask:

> How can I persist to-do items so they remain on reload?

The assistant might suggest using a database or a simple file. Perhaps it points out that Bolt integrates with Supabase for persistence. As a beginner, maybe a full database is too much, so you decide to keep it simple and use local storage in the browser. You then prompt Bolt to implement that (or do it yourself, if you're comfortable).

Step by step, you've debugged and improved the app: each failure or missing piece has guided you to the next fix.

By approaching debugging as a sequence of small investigations and fixes, you've not only gotten the app to work, but you've also learned *why* it works. Every time you see an error and collaborate with Bolt to solve it, you gain insight. Remember, even though Bolt writes the code, you are the problem-solver guiding it. In the end, debugging in Bolt is about communication: interpreting what the app is telling you, and clearly telling Bolt what to do in return.

Next, let's move on to uncovering some of Bolt's hidden superpowers that can make your development experience even smoother.

Lesser-Known Bolt Features

Bolt is more than just "enter prompt, get app." It offers a range of features and workflows that can turbocharge your productivity and expand what you can build. Many newcomers stick to the basics—writing prompts and using the rollback feature when needed—but there's a lot more you can do. This section explores some lesser-known (or just underutilized) Bolt features that will help you work smarter and push the platform to its full potential.

File Targeting and Locking

By default, Bolt's AI considers the entire project when making changes. But sometimes you want to direct its focus or protect certain code. Bolt's code editor offers Target and Lock features to give you fine-grained control. If you right-click a file, you'll see options like "Target file" and "Lock file." (See Figure 12-2 for a screenshot of these options.)

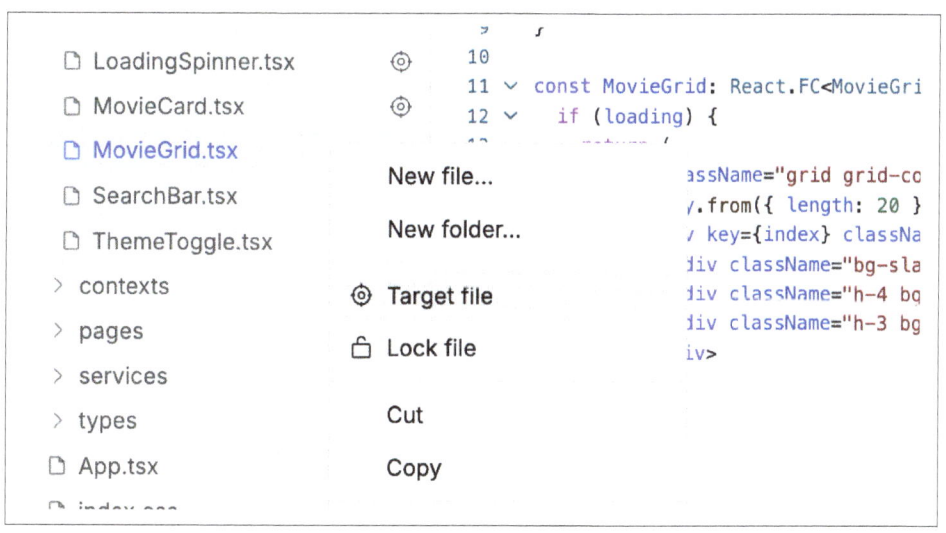

Figure 12-2. Options for targeting and locking files in Bolt

Selecting Target on a file (*https://oreil.ly/wIhB6*) tells Bolt to only modify that file (or set of files) in response to the next prompt. This is useful when you know exactly where a change needs to occur. For example, if you want to tweak the *Header.jsx* component, you can target it, then say:

> Make the header background animated on scroll.

Bolt will then confine its edits to *Header.jsx* (and perhaps related CSS files) rather than touching unrelated parts of the project. This prevents the AI from roaming and potentially introducing side effects elsewhere.

Conversely, selecting Lock on a file (*https://oreil.ly/VaJq8*) prevents the AI from making any changes to that file. The locked file becomes read-only, from the AI's perspective. This is great when you have critical code working correctly and you don't want it altered. For instance, if Bolt generates a complex utility module that finally works after much tweaking, you might lock it before moving on so that future prompts don't accidentally refactor or break it. You're essentially telling the AI, "hands off this piece." You can always unlock it later if needed.

These features are a bit hidden in the UI, but they can be productivity lifesavers. They allow a level of precision in AI-assisted coding that feels like managing a team: you can assign the AI to focus on one file or tell it to leave something alone, similar to how a senior dev might tell a junior dev, "Don't touch the payment module—just work on the UI." For beginners, using targeting can also help you learn by focusing changes: it forces you to think, "which file should this change be in?" That's a good habit for understanding project structures.

Ignoring Files: Advanced Context Management

For those pushing Bolt to its limits, there's a highly advanced feature (*https://oreil.ly/4zx_m*) to control what the AI "sees" in the project. In every Bolt project (which is actually powered by StackBlitz), there is a hidden folder named *.bolt*. Inside it is a *.bolt/ignore* file (similar to a *gitignore* file) that lists files and directories to exclude from the AI's context. If you open your project in StackBlitz, you can edit this file to list files that Bolt's AI should ignore.

Why do this? As your project grows, the AI has to read more code with each prompt, using up tokens and possibly getting distracted by irrelevant parts. Ignoring large or unimportant files can free up space in the AI's context window and improve performance. For instance, you might ignore autogenerated files, large data files, or library code that you don't need the AI to consider.

Ignoring files is powerful but risky. The documentation warns that it's for "advanced users" and that hiding files can have "unintended consequences": namely, the AI might try to use something that it now can't see and get confused. So use it sparingly. For instance, if your project includes a huge library or a lot of content that's blowing up the token count, you can ignore those to focus on the main app logic. Just remember to reopen the project in Bolt after editing the ignore file, so the changes take effect.

Importing and Integrating with External Tools

Bolt isn't a closed island; it plays well with other tools, which can be a huge boost. You've already seen how Bolt integrates with Supabase (Chapters 6 and 8), Netlify (Chapter 7), and Figma (Chapter 9).

Another notable integration is with GitHub (*https://oreil.ly/oSEsG*) (see Chapter 10 for a detailed overview). You can take any public GitHub repository and open it in Bolt to start interacting with it. Simply append the GitHub repo's URL to *bolt.new/* in your browser. For example, going to *https://bolt.new/github.com/someuser/someproject* will load that project's code into Bolt.

This is a killer feature for experimenting with open source projects or using Bolt to refactor or extend an existing codebase. If you find some boilerplate code you like on GitHub, you can bring it into Bolt and then prompt the AI to modify it. This effectively combines the vast wealth of open source templates with Bolt's AI power. As I write this in summer 2025, Bolt only supports public repos and read-only from GitHub. You'll still need to download and push changes back to GitHub manually if you want to save them, but it's fantastic for quick prototyping or learning from others' code.

As we explored in-depth in Chapter 11, Bolt's integration with Expo (*https://oreil.ly/bS8Xi*) allows you to build full-featured mobile apps for iOS and Android. This powerful capability transforms Bolt from a web-only tool into a cross-platform development environment.

Bolt will scaffold a React Native app. It runs an Expo dev server in the WebContainer, and you can preview it on the web or get a QR code for the Expo Go app.

While the development process in Bolt is similar (chat and code), deploying mobile apps has extra steps, such as using Expo's EAS (Expo Application Services) for cloud builds and app store deployment. The key takeaway: Bolt isn't just for websites. If you have a mobile app idea, you can prototype it here, too, which is pretty extraordinary. This is an underutilized capability—many people don't realize they can target multiple platforms from Bolt.

Chrome Extensions: Supercharge and Snippets

Beyond the web app itself, Bolt offers two Chrome extensions that extend its capabilities. Supercharge (*https://superchargebolt.com*) (released in late 2024) is designed to "supercharge your development workflow." This extension adds a sidebar to Bolt with prompt templates, quick-insert design components, and usage statistics. It's particularly useful for reducing token consumption by providing ready-made prompts and speeding up repetitive actions. Think of it as having a library of prewritten instructions that you can customize rather than typing everything from scratch.

Snippets (*https://oreil.ly/VUUl5*) acts as a bridge between your local development environment and Bolt's AI assistance. With this extension, you can highlight code in VSCode, on Stack Overflow, or any webpage and quickly send it to Bolt for analysis or modification. It also lets you organize personal snippet libraries and insert them into Bolt with a simple / command. For example, if you're debugging code locally and get stuck, you can highlight the problematic function and send it to Bolt without copy-pasting.

These extensions are optional but show how Bolt's ecosystem is expanding to meet developers where they work, whether that's speeding up common tasks or bridging the gap between local and cloud development.

Real-World Examples of Hidden Features

To ground these features in reality, let's run through a quick scenario combining a few of the features you've just learned about. Imagine you have a project that Bolt initially created, and you've been adding features. It's gotten pretty large, with lots of components and maybe some markdown files for content. You notice Bolt's responses getting slower, and sometimes it seems to be forgetting earlier context—a sign that you're hitting its context window limits. Here's how you could apply some of these advanced features:

Use .bolt/ignore
> You decide to exclude the *node_modules* and some large JSON data files from context. You open in StackBlitz, edit *.bolt/ignore* to list those directories, and reopen in Bolt. Now the AI has less to chew on each prompt, which should make it more responsive.

Lock stable files
> You've debugged and perfected your auth logic in *auth.js*: it's critical, and it works. You lock it so Bolt won't change it while you focus on something else. Now you can prompt Bolt to implement a new feature (say, a profile page) without any risk that it could mess up your auth code while doing so.

Import a design
> Your designer shares a Figma link for a fancy new settings page. Instead of hand-coding the UI, you import the design from Figma with a frame URL, just like you did in Chapter 9. Bolt generates the corresponding React components and CSS for the design, and you have a styled page.

Ask Discussion Mode
> After importing and implementing the design, you see that it's beautiful but static. You want the settings form to actually save users' preferences. You're not sure of the best way to store user settings in a React app with Bolt, so you go into Discussion Mode and ask:

What's a good way to store user preferences (like dark mode on/off) in this Bolt.new app?

The AI suggests a plan to use `localStorage` for instant toggling and save to Supabase for long-term storage. You click "Implement this plan," and Bolt adds the code to toggle the theme, with a context provider, and saves the setting.

Deploy and share
Finally, you deploy the app via Netlify integration (like you did in Chapter 7).

Make changes
Later, you realize the app needs a small tweak, but you're away from your computer. Because the project is stored in your Bolt/StackBlitz account, you can log in from any browser, even on another machine, and access it. All of your Bolt chats and projects are visible under your StackBlitz account's Bolt collection. This feature is often overlooked. There's no need to carry code or set up a dev environment; your project lives in the cloud, and you can run it from anywhere.

As you can see, Bolt's lesser-known features empower you to do far more than work with basic prompts. They help you bridge gaps—like getting help on a bug or focusing the AI on specific files—making the development process more efficient and enjoyable. Part of becoming an "advanced" Bolt user is remembering that you have these tools at your disposal. Next time you're building with Bolt, take a moment to explore the UI menus or the docs; you might discover a feature that saves you an hour of work or teaches you something new.

Now that you're armed with robust debugging skills and knowledge of Bolt's special features, let's turn to one of Bolt's most revolutionary aspects: how it runs and manages backend code right in your browser.

Building Full Stack (Backend-Powered) Apps in Bolt

This section is aimed at readers with some programming experience who are ready to explore backend development. If you're brand-new to coding, you might want to bookmark this section and return after gaining more familiarity with JavaScript.

With backend capabilities at your fingertips, you can build truly full stack applications, including:

APIs and microservices
In earlier chapters, we made API calls directly from the browser using `fetch()`— this exposed API keys in the frontend code and limited what processing we could do. Creating server-side endpoints changes the game entirely. You can create RESTful routes or GraphQL endpoints in Bolt's Node environment. For example, you could prompt:

> Create an Express endpoint */api/weather* that fetches weather from OpenWeather API and returns the result.

Bolt will likely add an Express or Next.js API route, which, when called, performs that fetch server-side. This means your API key stays hidden on the server, you can add caching or rate limiting, and you can process the data before sending it to the frontend. Your frontend can then use the response. Essentially, Bolt lets you simulate having a backend server for your app, which is fantastic for learning client-server interactions or offloading tasks from the frontend.

Server-side rendering (SSR) and frameworks

Server-side rendering (SSR) means your web framework generates HTML on the server before sending it to the browser rather than having the browser build everything with JavaScript. This improves SEO and initial page load times. Modern frameworks like Next.js and Nuxt (Vue) have a server component for SSR or API routes. Bolt's environment can run these seamlessly. A Next.js app in Bolt will run its Node server for serving pages. You can experiment with SSR, knowing that it's truly running a server in that tab. This means beginners can dip their toes into full stack frameworks without setting up anything locally. If you're building a Nuxt blog, Bolt can handle both frontend UI generation and backend API management in one place.

Databases and storage

While you can't run, say, a full Postgres DB in WebContainer (not yet, anyway), Bolt covers this via its cloud integrations. Supabase provides a database, auth, and storage that your Bolt app can talk to over the internet. Bolt even helps set up the SDK keys, etc., in the project if you prompt for it. For lightweight needs, you could also use file-based storage in the WebContainer (since it has a virtual filesystem). For instance, an Express app could write to a JSON file to store data. However, remember that the WebContainer filesystem resets when you refresh the browser tab (it's ephemeral unless you download the project). So for persistence, a cloud database (or browser local storage for frontend) would be better.

Background jobs and scripts

It's not just servers: you can use Bolt to run one-off Node scripts too. Say you prompt:

> Generate a sitemap.xml by scanning all pages.

Bolt can write a Node script, execute it in the container, and produce a file. The environment comes with a shell, so the AI can run commands like `npm run build` or `node scripts/migrate.js` as needed. This blurs the line between coding and DevOps: you have the power of a miniserver at your disposal.

It does have one limitation: WebContainer doesn't support long-running processes that require a persistent connection outside, like a direct database socket, or things like spawning child OS processes. It's a Node sandbox but somewhat contained in what it can do. Still, it covers the vast majority of JavaScript use cases.

Best Practices for Leveraging Backend Power

Knowing you *can* run backends is one thing. Knowing how to use this power effectively is another, especially if you're new to server-side programming. Here are some tips:

Use familiar frameworks

If you don't know much Node.js, let Bolt handle it via frameworks. For example, ask for a simple Express setup or use Next.js API routes:

> Set up an Express server with a */api/hello* route returning "Hello world."

Bolt will scaffold the conventions, giving you a starting point, so you can focus on the logic. Once Bolt creates it, try modifying the response or adding another route by prompting. This iterative building teaches you backend basics in context.

Keep security in mind

The sandbox protects your machine, but you should still code responsibly. For instance, if you use API keys for external services, avoid printing them or exposing them in the frontend. Bolt doesn't have a secrets manager per se, but you can store keys in environment variables if the framework supports it. (Next.js uses *.env* files, which you could have Bolt set). When it comes to secrets, always treat your Bolt project as public (even though it's private by default) and don't commit any keys you can't revoke.

Leverage logs

Like in frontend debugging, `console.log` is your friend server-side. If you create an API endpoint and it's not working as expected, add logs in the code or prompt Bolt:

> Add logging to the */api/hello* route to print the request body.

Then trigger that route, maybe by using the frontend or a tool like `fetch` in the console, and check Bolt's console output. Yes, Bolt's interface or your browser DevTools console will show server `console.log` output, too, often in a special pane; errors are usually annotated in the chat. This way, you can see what's happening on the "server" as it runs, which is crucial for understanding things like request data and error traces.

Try the app offline

One awesome aspect of WebContainers is that after everything loads, it can work offline (*https://oreil.ly/A3SYN*) for static files or even API routes that don't need external access. This isn't a feature you toggle; it's just a byproduct of running in the browser. For example, if you have a purely self-contained app (with no external API calls), you could lose your internet connection and the app would still function in that open tab. This shows how blurry the boundary between frontend and backend is—it's all just in-browser. It also highlights that, to the browser, your Node server is just another script running. It doesn't differentiate between serving an API or manipulating the DOM (Document Object Model); both can be debugged with the same tools.

Respect limits

While it's tempting to run heavy servers, remember that WebContainer has limits. It's perfect for prototyping, learning, and even small-scale apps. But if you try to do something like video encoding or running a machine-learning model on it, you'll hit performance bottlenecks or memory limits quickly.

Also, it's single-user—it's not like a cloud server that can handle multiple concurrent clients nicely. If you deploy the app via Netlify, Netlify will handle hosting a proper backend (though it typically only hosts frontends; for backends, you'd deploy to other services or use serverless functions). The key point: use the backend in Bolt to develop and test full stack logic, but for production, move heavy backends to a dedicated environment. For learning and prototyping, though, Bolt's backend is more than sufficient.

Another limitation: if the Node library uses some native module or unsupported Node API, it might fail in WebContainer. WebContainers cover a lot of Node.js APIs but not 100%. If you hit an issue like "Unsupported module," you might need a workaround (for example, some file-system or network operations might not be allowed). The vast majority of web-centric libraries (like HTTP requests and processing data) will work fine.

Use it to learn Node.js

If you're a beginner, Bolt can be a great sandbox to learn backend JavaScript. You can ask it to show you examples or create small servers and then inspect the code.

Because it's conversational, you can inquire:

> Explain how this Express middleware works.

In Discussion Mode, the AI will break down the backend code it wrote for you, teaching you concepts as you go. Then you can tweak the code and see what happens instantly. It's a far cry from the days of having to set up Node, an editor, Postman, and so on just to toy with a backend concept.

Example: Running a Backend Task in Bolt

Suppose you want to add a contact form to your Bolt-generated React site. You need a backend route to email the form details, since you don't want to expose email service credentials on the frontend. In Bolt, you prompt:

> Add a backend function that sends an email via SendGrid when the contact form is submitted.

Bolt adds a new API route (let's say it chooses to create */api/sendEmail*) and writes code to use SendGrid's Node library. It will `npm install` @sendgrid/mail behind the scenes. The code will likely include an API key for SendGrid; Bolt might ask you for your SendGrid API key. You supply it, maybe storing it in an *.env* file that Bolt creates.

Now, when you fill and submit the form in the web app, the frontend will call `/api/sendEmail` (Bolt will generally wire this up in the form handler). The Node code runs in WebContainer, contacts SendGrid, and sends the email out. You get a success response, and perhaps Bolt logs "Email sent" in the console.

This is an example of end-to-end, full stack development: a frontend form, backend email logic, and an external API call. You've just integrated an external service with a backend function, all from a browser tab, with Bolt coordinating all of it.

Keep in mind that any secrets (like your SendGrid key) live in your project code. Bolt's environment isn't publicly accessible to others, but if you share your project, someone could see it. So rotate any keys you use in demos, and don't share your Bolt project URL if it contains sensitive info.

Deploying and Exporting Your Backend

When you're ready to deploy the full app, remember that Netlify (Bolt's default) is a static host that also offers serverless functions. Serverless functions are small pieces of backend code that run on demand without needing a traditional always-on server— they spin up when called, execute your code, and shut down, making them cost-effective and scalable. Bolt might automatically convert your API routes to Netlify Functions when you deploy. If not, you could manually move the code or download the project and run it on a Node server of your own or another platform. The code Bolt produced is just Node/Express or Next.js code—you can treat it like any other project. For example, you could take a Bolt Next.js project and deploy to Vercel easily.

What you build and test in WebContainer will behave the same on a real server, since WebContainer is designed to mimic Node closely. One subtle difference is performance: WebContainer might be a tad slower or more constrained, so if it works there, it'll likely work better on a proper Node environment.

Final Thoughts on Backend in Bolt

For beginners and junior developers, Bolt's backend capabilities are an invitation to explore the server side without fear. You can gradually transition from just tweaking the UI to writing API endpoints, doing database ops, and more, all within a familiar setting that gives you immediate feedback. It lowers the barrier to entry for full stack development. By practicing in Bolt's sandbox, you'll gain skills applicable to any Node.js environment. You'll also appreciate the convenience of having one continuous workflow, with no context switching between frontend and backend.

To use this power safely, avoid running code that you don't understand. Bolt's AI won't write malicious code on purpose, but if you integrate third-party examples, be cautious. Always test things thoroughly in the preview. If something might have side effects, like sending emails or charging a payment, maybe use test credentials or a safe mode first. Normal good development practices apply—Bolt just makes the iteration loop much faster.

In summary, WebContainers turn your browser into a full stack playground. Bolt capitalizes on this to give you an all-in-one dev and runtime. By understanding how to command the backend side of Bolt—writing server code via prompts, debugging it, and integrating services—you elevate your capabilities from frontend developer to true full stack developer. And you've done so with minimal setup, focusing on learning and building rather than configuring.

As you continue using Bolt, push the boundaries of what you build: try adding a custom Node module, or build a small API-only service with it. You'll find that the skills translate to conventional development as well. Bolt's magic is making the complex world of full stack app development *accessible*—empowering you to create complete applications through prompts, from database to browser.

By leveraging these advanced tools, you've effectively transformed your browser into a powerful development powerhouse. You have the instant feedback of StackBlitz and the robust capabilities of a full dev environment. Now, let's wrap up everything we've learned and look at the journey you've taken from Bolt to StackBlitz.

Summary

Congratulations on making it through this deep dive into StackBlitz! Let's take a moment to reflect on what we've covered and why it matters.

At the start, you had a movie app magically generated by Bolt—a quick start, thanks to AI. Through this book, you stepped out of that magic box and into the workshop of StackBlitz, where you gained hands-on experience with your project. You learned what StackBlitz is: an online development environment that's as immediate and convenient as Bolt's generation but with the granularity and control that only manual coding can provide.

We walked through exporting your project from Bolt to StackBlitz, a simple yet pivotal step that opened up your ability to tinker freely. You then acclimated to the StackBlitz editor, discovering how it puts all the tools at your fingertips. It might have felt like a lot at first, but by incrementally exploring and making small changes, you've seen that coding is an iterative, creative process. Each edit and reload deepens your understanding.

Comparing Bolt's AI-driven workflow to your new manual approach highlights a key lesson: there's great power in *both* methods. Bolt gave you speed and a safety net when you were starting from scratch; StackBlitz gives you precision and learning as you move forward, gaining confidence in reading and writing code directly. They're not mutually exclusive—they're complementary.

Enhancing the TMDB app was a chance to spread your wings. You added features, improved the interface, maybe even dipped into backend logic. These enhancements weren't just about making the app cooler (though that's a nice outcome)—they were about empowering you to build whatever you imagine. By going through the exercise of adding a search bar or handling an API error, you leveled up your skills in understanding APIs, UI events, and error handling. By considering a backend or integrating new libraries, you glimpsed the wider world of full stack development—all within the friendly confines of StackBlitz.

The advanced tooling in StackBlitz, like the terminal and GitHub integration, shows that this platform isn't a toy: it's capable of real-world development workflows. You've essentially performed the tasks of professional developers: managing dependencies, running servers, using version control, and collaborating via GitHub. And you did it without leaving your browser or installing anything on your machine! That's a testament to how far development environments have come. You should feel proud. You've gone from an idea ("movie app with TMDB data") to an AI-generated solution, then to truly owning the project by manually extending and refining it.

Moving forward, you can use this book as both a tutorial and a reference. If you forget how to do something—say, pushing to GitHub or what steps to export from

Bolt—you can flip to that chapter and review the steps. If you're starting a *new* project, you might even use Bolt to scaffold it, then recall from this guide how to jump into StackBlitz to customize it.

Today it's a movie app; tomorrow it could be anything—a personal blog, a small ecommerce demo, a game, or an inventory tool for work. Bolt can help kickstart many types of projects, and StackBlitz can be your development playground and workshop to bring them to life. As you grow more confident, you might transition to local development environments or other cloud IDEs, but the concepts remain similar. The fundamental skills you've picked up—editing code, understanding project structure, debugging, using terminals and version control—will serve you in countless scenarios.

Learning to code (and becoming proficient) is a continuous journey. Embrace both the convenience of AI helpers and the depth of manual coding. Use analogies, break problems into smaller pieces (like we did with feature enhancements), and don't be afraid to consult documentation and communities when you're stuck. The web development community is vast and supportive—and now you're part of it! Keep experimenting, keep building, and, most importantly, have fun on your coding adventures.

Thanks for reading, and happy coding in the cloud!

Index

About the Author

Addy Osmani is a senior engineering leader at Google, where he works on developer experience, performance, and AI-powered software development tools. He has 25 years of industry experience building web technologies and has authored multiple books on software engineering best practices.

He has worked extensively with AI-driven developer tools, testing and evaluating emerging platforms like GitHub Copilot, OpenAI Codex, v0.dev, Cursor, and Cline. His writing on AI-assisted software development has influenced thousands of developers, and his leadership at Google Chrome has helped shape the future of web performance and AI-augmented developer workflows.

This book distills his deep expertise in software engineering and his hands-on experience with AI-powered coding assistants, offering developers practical strategies to integrate AI into their daily workflow and adapt to the rapidly changing landscape of software development.

Colophon

The animal on the cover of *Building Web Apps with Bolt* is a caracal (*Caracal caracal*), a wild cat native to Africa. The caracal is also known as the desert lynx. These cats thrive in forest, savanna, shrubland, grassland, and desert environments. The species also ranges across the Middle East and India.

Caracals have distinctive long, black tufts of fur atop their ears, dramatic dark facial markings, and an otherwise solid reddish-gold coat. Adults are typically 24–42 inches long, about 18 inches tall, and 13–44 pounds, with females on the smaller side. They hunt a variety of prey by night, including mongooses, rodents, dik-diks, and monkeys. Caracals can run up to 50 miles per hour and leap up to 10 feet; they have been seen doing so to swat at birds in flight.

The IUCN rates the caracal's conservation status as "Least Concern," but this assessment is over 10 years old at the time of this book's publication and it needs updating. Many of the animals on O'Reilly covers are endangered; all of them are important to the world.

The cover illustration is by José Marzan Jr., based on an antique line engraving from *Natural History of Animals*. The series design is by Edie Freedman, Ellie Volckhausen, and Karen Montgomery. The cover fonts are Gilroy Semibold and Guardian Sans. The text font is Adobe Minion Pro; the heading font is Adobe Myriad Condensed; and the code font is Dalton Maag's Ubuntu Mono.

O'REILLY®

Learn from experts.
Become one yourself.

60,000+ titles | Live events with experts | Role-based courses
Interactive learning | Certification preparation

 **Try the O'Reilly learning platform
free for 10 days.**

www.ingramcontent.com/pod-product-compliance
Lightning Source LLC
Jackson TN
JSHW052130070925
90580JS00013B/105